China in the WTO

Also by Carlos A. Magariños

REFORMING THE UN SYSTEM: UNIDO's Need-Driven Model (*with George Assaf, Sanjaya Lall, John D.-Martinussen, Rubens Ricupero and Francisco C. Sercovich*)

GEARING UP FOR A NEW DEVELOPMENT AGENDA – MARGINALIZATION VS. PROSPERITY: How to Improve and Spread the Gains of Globalization (*with Francisco C. Sercovich*)

THE ROLE OF THE STATE AND INDUSTRIAL POLICY IN THE 1990s (*with the collaboration of José L. Díaz. Pérez and Pablo Sierra*)

Also by Francisco C. Sercovich

REFORMING THE UN SYSTEM: UNIDO's Need-Driven Model (*with Carlos A. Magariños, George Assaf, Sanjaya Lall, John D.-Martinussen and Rubens Ricupero*)

GEARING UP FOR A NEW DEVELOPMENT AGENDA – MARGINALIZATION VS. PROSPERITY: How to Improve and Spread the Gains of Globalization (*with Carlos A. Magariños*)

COMPETITION AND THE WORLD ECONOMY: Comparing Industrial Development Policies in Developing and Transition Economies (*with Choong-Yong Ahn, Claudio Frischtak, Mojmir Mrak, Herman Muegge, Wilson Peres and Samuel Wangwe*)

FOREIGN TECHNOLOGY IN ARGENTINE INDUSTRY (in Spanish)

China in the WTO

The Birth of a New Catching-Up Strategy

Edited by

Carlos A. Magariños
Director-General, UNIDO
Chair, United Nations High-Level Committee on Programmes

Long Yongtu
China's Vice-Minister of Trade and Chief WTO Negotiator

and

Francisco C. Sercovich
Senior Policy Advisor to the Director-General, UNIDO

**UNITED NATIONS INDUSTRIAL
DEVELOPMENT ORGANIZATION**

382.92
C 539

© United Nations Industrial Development Organization 2002

All rights reserved. No reproduction, copy or transmission of this
publication may be made without written permission.

No paragraph of this publication may be reproduced, copied or transmitted
save with written permission or in accordance with the provisions of the
Copyright, Designs and Patents Act 1988, or under the terms of any licence
permitting limited copying issued by the Copyright Licensing Agency, 90
Tottenham Court Road, London W1T 4LP.

Any person who does any unauthorised act in relation to this publication
may be liable to criminal prosecution and civil claims for damages.

The authors have asserted their rights to be identified as the authors of
this work in accordance with the Copyright, Designs and Patents Act 1988.

First published 2002 by
PALGRAVE MACMILLAN
Houndmills, Basingstoke, Hampshire RG21 6XS and
175 Fifth Avenue, New York, N.Y. 10010
Companies and representatives throughout the world

PALGRAVE MACMILLAN is the global academic imprint of the Palgrave
Macmillan division of St. Martin's Press, LLC and of Palgrave Macmillan Ltd.
Macmillan® is a registered trademark in the United States, United Kingdom
and other countries. Palgrave is a registered trademark in the European
Union and other countries.

ISBN 0–333–99930–4

This book is printed on paper suitable for recycling and made from fully
managed and sustained forest sources.

A catalogue record for this book is available from the British Library.

MK Library of Congress Cataloging-in-Publication Data

China in the WTO / edited by Carlos A. Magariños, Long Yongtu, and
Francisco C. Sercovich.
        p. cm.
    "UNIDO."
    Includes papers from a forum took place on Dec. 4–5 2000 in Shanghai.
    Includes bibliographical references and indexes.
    ISBN 0–333–99930–4 (cloth)
      1. World Trade Organization – China. 2. China – Commercial policy.
    3. China – Foreign economic relations – Developing countries.
    4. Developing countries – Foreign economic relations – China.
    5. China – Economic conditions – 2000– I. Magariños, Carlos A. II. Long,
    Yongtu, 1943– III. Sercovich, Francisco Colman. IV. United Nations
    Industrial Development Organization.

    HF1385 .C477 2002
    382'.92'0951–dc21   2002073539

10   9   8   7   6   5   4   3   2   1
11   10   09   08   07   06   05   04   03   02

Printed and bound in Great Britain by
Antony Rowe Ltd, Chippenham and Eastbourne

Contents

University Libraries
Carnegie Mellon University
Pittsburgh PA 15213-3890

List of Boxes, Tables and Figures

Figures

List of the Contributors

Albaladejo, Manuel	Researcher, University of Oxford, Centre for International Development
Chae, Wook	Research Fellow, Korea Institute for International Economic Policy, Republic of Korea
Han, Hongyul	Associate Professor, Department of Economics, Hanyang University, Republic of Korea
Lall, Sanjaya	Professor, Oxford University
Luken, Ralph A.	Senior Industrial Development Officer, UNIDO
Margariños, Carlos A.	Director-General, UNIDO and Chair, United Nations High-Level Committee on Programmes
Nogués, Julio J.	Consultant, UNIDO
Sercovich, Francisco C.	Senior Policy Adviser to the Director-General, UNIDO
Panitchpakdi, Supachai	Director-General designate of the WTO
van der Tak, Casper	Consultant, UNIDO
Yongtu, Long	China's Vice-Minister of Trade and Chief WTO Negotiator

The views expressed in this publication are those of the authors and do not necessarily reflect the views of the Secretariat of the United Nations Industrial Development Organization. The description and classifications of countries and territories used, and the arrangements of the material, do not imply the expression of any opinion whatsoever on the part of the Secretariat concerning the legal status of any country, territory, city or area, or of its authorities, concerning the delimitation of its frontiers or boundaries, or regarding its economic system or degree of development. Designations such as 'developed', 'industrialized' and 'developing' are intended for statistical convenience and do not necessarily express a judgement about the stage reached by a particular country or area in the development process. Mention of firm names and commercial products does not imply the endorsement of the United Nations Industrial Development Organization.

Bk Title !

Foreword

Carlos A. Magariños

NIA

Both in length and intricacy, the history of this book pales by comparison with that of the implementation of China's bold decision to join the World Trade Organization – a decision that took 15 years of tough negotiations on multiple tracks before a successful outcome was ultimately reached. But, all the same, this book does have a history.

By early May 2000, when China was entering the final stage of negotiations, I led an official mission to Beijing, Shanghai and Xiang. At a dinner offered by Mr Long Yongtu, China's Vice-Minister of Trade and Chief Negotiator before the WTO, we addressed China's accession to the multilateral trade body, among other issues. This exchange captured my imagination, giving birth to the idea of organizing a Regional Forum to assess this particular topic and draw policy conclusions. The Forum took place on 4–5 December 2000 in Shanghai. My intention was to zero-in on a number of dimensions pertaining to what, in my view, clearly marked a watershed in the evolution of the multilateral trade system – one perhaps as significant in itself as an entire round of trade negotiations. Among such dimensions, at the core of my concerns was the potential impact of China's WTO entry on the competitive standing of other emerging Asian economies and on the developing world at large.

Later, when I examined the proceedings of the Forum with my friend and colleague Francisco Sercovich, we arrived at the conclusion that the value and originality of the material warranted publishing a book on the subject. As is usually the case, our original idea was outgrown by events. Because of his unique experience and mastery of the subject, I invited Mr Long Yongtu to join us as co-editor and contribute with two key chapters of the book – as suggested by Palgrave Macmillan. Additional chapters were also requested from other experts. In a nutshell, we ended up with having all chapters in the book expressly written for it, save for two – those by Mr Supachai Panitchpakdi, Director-General designate of the WTO and by Korean Republic researchers Chae Wook and Han Hongyul, which were originally presented at UNIDO's Shanghai Forum and are included here with minor changes.

Among the great variety of challenges arising from China's accession to the WTO, the following warrant particular attention. First, China confronts the three-pronged challenge of sustaining its growth momentum at a rate high enough to offer productive outlet to the large contingents of new entrants to the job market; complying with the WTO agreements; and keeping up with economic opening and technological catch-up. Secondly, trade relations between China and its commercial partners, both in the developed and developing worlds, need to be deepened in the context of a fair and transparent reciprocal treatment. And thirdly, the multilateral trade system requires taking advantage of China's ascription to the multilateral trade rules in order to build bridges between the agendas pursued by developed and developing countries and thus help to overcome actual and potential fissures in international trade relations.

One of the most valuable lessons from the last 50 years of economic history is that such things as the opening of the economy, fiscal balance and macroeconomic stability are key to growth – and vice versa. However, they are not sufficient, neither should they be taken as mantras, since in and of themselves, they fall short of addressing issues of equity and efficiency. Although they play an important role in achieving progress and prosperity, they are compatible with different distributional patterns both nationally and internationally, including those that segregate high concentration of wealth, on the one hand, and extend poverty, on the other. This problem is not limited just to the developing countries. Social and human deprivation also prevails in large sections of developed country societies.

I believe that the key challenge faced by the international community is not how to foster wealth creation where it already exists, but how to do it where it does not. And here is where China offers an inspiring example with its home-growth policies to switch from a command economy to a market economy within just over a generation.

In historical perspective, development through rapid economic and social change and massive wealth creation are rather recent achievements of civilization. Prior civilizations did produce important advances in science, technology, trade and entrepreneurship, but the impact of these achievements on wealth creation, important as it was, proved not to be sustainable. The systematic use of scientific and technological innovation in economic activity during recent times is an important condition for sustainability. But it does not suffice either. Breaking the negative links between equity and efficiency is another key condition. Indeed, civilization is at the dawn of development, whose mastery is a task that still remains largely ahead of us. China has a key contribution to make to this goal.

Acknowledgements

Thanks are due to the following UNIDO staff from the Asia and the Pacific Bureau: J.-W. Suh, Director; S. Miranda-da-Cruz, UNIDO Representative in China; C. Scaratti, UNIDO Representative in Thailand; and C.-P. Chua, Field Operations Officer, for their valuable cooperation. D. Liang, Director of the Industrial Promotion and Technology Branch also provided kind assistance. Nicola Viinikka, Senior Editor of Palgrave, gave continuous support to the project. E. Crawley did the style editing. M.-A. Yap was responsible for the copy-editing.

List of Abbreviations and Acronyms

AP	Asia-Pacific
ASEAN	Association of Southeast Asian Nations
ATC	Agreement on Textiles and Clothing
ATCA	Agreement on Trade in Civil Aircraft
BIT	bilateral investment treaties
CESTT	Center for Environmentally Sound Technology Transfer
CGE	Computable General Equilibrium
CMS	constant market analysis
CPA	Certified Public Accountants
CPC	Communist Party of China
CTE	Committee on Trade and Environment
DSM	Dispute Settlement Mechanism
ECLAC	Economic Commission for Latin America and the Caribbean
EIAs	Environmental Impact Assessments
EIU	Economics Intelligence Unit
EKC	Environmental Kuznets Curve
EMIT	Environment Measures and International Trade
EMS	Environmental Management Systems
EPB	Environmental Protection Bureau
ESTs	environmentally sound technologies
EU	European Union
FDI	foreign direct investment
FTAA	Free Trade Agreement of the Americas
FYP	Five-Year Plan
GATT	General Agreement on Tariffs and Trade
GDP	gross domestic product
GNP	gross national product
HS	Harmonized System
HT	high technology manufactures
ICT	information and communications technologies
ILO	International Labor Organization
IPPS	Industrial Pollution Projection System
IPR	intellectual property rights

ISO	International Standard Organization
IT	information technology
ITA	Information Technology Agreement
LDCs	least developed countries
LT	low technology manufactures
MFA	Multi-Fiber Agreement
MFN	most-favoured-nation
MHT	medium and high technology
MNCs	multinational companies
MOFTEC	Ministry of Foreign Trade and Economic Cooperation, China
MT	medium technology manufactures
MVA	manufacturing value added
NAFTA	North American Free Trade Association
NGOs	non-governmental organizations
NIE	newly industrialized economies
NPC	National People's Congress
NTBs	non-tariff barriers
OECD	Organization for Economic Cooperation and Development
OEM	original equipment manufacture
PCMC	para-chloro-meta-cresol
PCP	pentachlorophenol
PCS	personal communication services
PLS	pollution levy system
PNTR	Permanent Normal Trade Relations
PRCEE	Policy Research Center for Environment and Economy
PROPER	Program for Pollution Control Evaluation and Rating
R&D	research and development
RB	resource-based manufactures
RCA	revealed comparative advantage
S&T	science and technology
SEPA	State Environmental Protection Administration
SEZ	Special Economic Zones
SIC	Standard Industrial Classification
SITC	Standard International Trade Classification
SME	small and medium-sized enterprise
SO$_2$	sulphur dioxide
SOEs	state-owned enterprises
SPS	Sanitary and Phytosanitary
SSA	Sub-Saharan Africa

TBT	Technical Barriers to Trade
TCMTB	thiocyanatomethylbenzothiazole
TFP	total factor productivity
TNCs	transnational corporations
TPA	Trade Promotion Act
TRIMs	Trade-Related Investment Measures
TRIP	Trade-Related Industrial Property
TRQ	tariff rate quota
TSP	total suspended particulates
TVEs	Town and Village Enterprises
UNCTAD	United Nations Conference on Trade and Development
UNDP	United Nations Development Programme
UNEP	United Nations Environmental Programme
UNIDO	United Nations Industrial Development Organization
UR	Uruguay Round
US	United States
USEPA	US Environmental Protection Agency
USITC	US International Trade Commission
USTPA	US Trade Promotion Action
WIPO	World Intellectual Property Organization
WTO	World Trade Organization

1
China's Accession to the WTO: an Overview of Domestic and External Implications

Carlos A. Magariños and Francisco C. Sercovich

P33 F14

019 F16

On 11 December 2001 China became the 143rd member of the World Trade Organization (WTO). This way, a 15 years-long quest came to an end, concluding the first chapter of a remarkably rich learning process for all parties concerned (Chapter 2 gives a first-hand, authoritative account from the Chinese perspective).[1] There can be little doubt that the implementation stage of the accession agreement, including both China's adaptation to WTO rules and WTO adaptation to its more universal membership base, although an unlikely subject for replication in the aggregate, will also be a rich source of lessons for the international community, particularly the developing countries.

WTO accession means for China a key step forward in its unprecedented strategy to catch up with the advanced industrial world by means of market socialism.[2] This way China legitimizes internationally its vocation to regain its place at the world technological and productivity frontier within the span of a few decades.[3] And it does so without adopting orthodox prescriptions, such as brisk capital account liberalization or privatization of its state-owned enterprises (SOEs).

The terms of China's accession to the WTO may be viewed as a deal whereby, for the sake of significant medium- and long-term mutual gains, China accepts the risks involved in limiting the degree of heterodoxy of its peculiar brand of catching up and China's trade partners take the risks entailed in trusting the ability of China's leadership to deliver on its commitments.

This is a high-stakes game for all concerned. The major risk incurred by China is the potentially disruptive social implications of carrying out, within a decade or so, the wholesale adaptation of its economic,

1

institutional and legal structure to a still untested brand of market-led competition. China's trade partners risk significant shifts in relative competitive advantage.[4]

China has reasserted its rights to considerable elbow-room in policy design and implementation. This does not mean that China has extracted undue unilateral advantages: on the contrary, the magnitude of the commitments made by China's leadership leaves it facing daunting challenges and risks. In addition, China is likely to pay a premium for choosing to catch up via market socialism rather than through market capitalism (see below).

The challenges ahead cannot be overstated. The terms of the agreement suggest China's self-confidence in the ability to draw on its manufacturing prowess to a much larger extent than before. This China will attempt to do by matching an enhanced innovative and technological capability with labour cost advantages that are unlikely to vanish in the near future.

Inward dimensions

China faces a wide variety of challenges in striving to promote national development and catch up with the industrial countries along an original track. WTO accession has already demanded and will continue to demand the deployment of enormous and highly qualified manpower resources. For instance, China must amend no less than 177 domestic laws and regulations regarding custom administration, foreign investment, intellectual property and services to ensure consistency with WTO obligations (see Chapter 2). These laws and regulations need to be properly revised and then passed by the National People's Congress (NPC). Judges have to be trained, the legal institutions and procedures need to ensure that the laws are fairly and impartially upheld and the legal judgements must be enforceable throughout the country.[5] In addition, there is the need to maintain the momentum of reform; address resource shortages, low productivity and quality deficiencies; reallocate a high percentage of the labour force; attend the needs of the social security, educational and science and technology (S&T) systems; correct regional unevenness and address deflationary pressures.[6]

Keeping up with continuous reform at the necessary speed, neither too fast nor too slow, will be particularly demanded if, as intended, it is to be based on innovative homegrown transitional institutional and policy devices. Most of the challenges involve taking entirely new approaches. Consider quality as a case in point: hitherto seen largely as a matter of enforcement, it will have to be viewed now as relating to exposure to competition and innovative performance. The Chinese leadership has a remarkable record at matching domestic needs and the reaping of world market opportunities. This ability will continue to be tested. Ingrained traits such as uneven market power, discretionary procurement policies and intra-domestic trade barriers slow down efficiency gains. These traits must now be uprooted. Appropriate ways must be found to develop a framework of regulations and incentives capable of promoting efficiency with equity while discouraging rent seeking.

The tenth Five-Year Plan (FYP) grants critical importance to productivity gains from reform and innovation. This will demand an extensive revision of economic incentives, institutions and legal as well as regulatory frameworks for the development of entrepreneurial skills, competition, financing, labour, social security and small- and medium-sized enterprise (SME) promotion. Let us focus on some of the most important medium-term challenges associated with accession.

Challenge 1: creating employment opportunities

China has a labour force of 700 million. If we add up the unemployed (estimated unofficially at about 10 per cent of the labour force), new entrants to the labour market and workers released by the agricultural sector, SOEs and Town and Village Enterprises (TVEs), it is clear that very large contingents will be seeking jobs within the next few years.[7] In a conservative estimate, the Chinese economy will need to create about twice as many jobs as it has been creating annually over the last few years – while it was growing at 8 per cent per year, not the 7 per cent envisaged by the tenth FYP for 2001–5. No fewer than 100 million jobs will have to be created during the current decade, mostly in urban areas (Dahlman and Aubert, 2001). Heavy industries (chemicals, metal products and machinery), which account for more than 56 per cent of total manufacturing employment, are unlikely to create a great deal of the additional jobs required – though they will certainly undergo substantial reshuffling and labour reallocation. High technology and advanced manufacturing activities may increase employment by up to 20–30 million during the current decade. This means that much of the remainder will have to come from the expansion of the formal and informal service sectors and other labour-intensive activities.

Labor-intensive industries account for more than 30 per cent of manufacturing employment. This share will most likely go up, matching expectations of a substantial growth in China's world market shares in these activities, particularly textiles and clothing (see below and Chapter 3; for a qualification *vis-à-vis* medium and high technology activities, see Chapter 4).

Overall, increases in the job creation potential will require the right mix of productivity growth, technological and quality upgrading and product/service diversification so as to conciliate gains in competitiveness with an enlarged labour base and a shifting skill mix. The development of a sound social, security and skill development infrastructure will also be required, particularly in view of the progressive ageing of the working population as a result of the one-child policy.

Challenge 2: keeping the pace of structural change and policy reform[8]

One of the keys to the successful structural transformation of the Chinese economy has been its ability to sustain a very high growth rate: an average of around 10 per cent per year from the late 1970s to the late 1990s. Most forecasts concur that, during the next decade, China will have to manage with a lower rate of growth, probably in the 6 to 7 per cent range. Even if this could be exceeded if the world economy improves, it may not be enough to make the task easier.

Moreover, the pattern of structural change ahead will be qualitatively different – less extensive but more focused. So far it has consisted largely of dismantling the command economy and extending the scope of the market economy. Although there is still a long way to go along these lines, attention will have to shift towards building market-supporting institutions, improving patterns of corporate governance, upgrading technology, management and skills and developing innovative capabilities. Three important gauges of structural change so far are:

1. The increased share of foreign trade in gross national product (GNP) from 16 per cent in 1980 to 41 per cent in 1999.
2. The fall in the primary sector's share from more than 70 per cent in 1978 to 50 per cent in the late 1990s.
3. The increase in industry share of employment from 17 per cent to 25 per cent during the same period.

The service sector has lagged remarkably behind in growth. Within the next few years it can be expected to become a key source of employment and, as importantly, a key provider of innovative and productivity enhancing inputs for industry. China has experienced an extraordinary growth of high technology manufacturing activities. In the 1980s and early 1990s, labour-intensive products such as toys, footwear and apparel (many relocated from Hong Kong SAR, China and Taiwan Province of China), were the most dynamic. From the early 1990s, though, dynamism began to be led by computer component manufacturing and an expanding range of high-tech hardware products (motherboards, monitors, etc.). By the mid-1990s China had already emerged as a significant supplier of finished computers. By 2000, two-fifths of all Taiwanese PCs were made in China, which was expected to replace Taiwan as the world's third largest manufacturer of information technology (IT) hardware by 2001. The range of high technology products within China's export mix will keep broadening, to include notebook computers and semi-conductor production (see Chapter 3 from the perspective of challenges posed to other developing Asia-Pacific (AP) countries).

Nevertheless, pockets of inefficiency still prevail in agriculture, industry (particularly the SOEs) and finance (burdened by non-performing loans).[9] These sectors will carry the brunt of the forthcoming transformation, along with major institutional and legal reforms, helped by the pull from new, state-of-the-art, dynamic activities.[10] So far, China has resorted to a number homegrown transitional policies and institutions to match equity with structural transformation by minimizing losers. The best known among such policies and institutions are:

1. The dual-track approach under which prices were liberalized only over and above plan prices and quotas. As the former grew at a much faster pace, the latter became an increasingly narrower part of the economy.
2. The rural TVEs, which are neither private nor owned by the national government.
3. A working fiscal federalism to provide economic incentives for provincial and local governments, which manage about 70 per cent of the national budget) (Qian, 2001).

By using such devices, China's leadership has been able to sort out what ex-ante would have been perceived as insurmountable quandaries. This ability is now being put to test again before an attentive world audience. WTO entry can be expected to mean a substantially heightened codification of the standards of behaviour of all economic agents, reducing the scope for discretional and unpredictable conduct and increasing transparency, accountability and equity.

Challenge 3: reducing regional and social inequalities

The growing gaps between urban and rural areas and between the coastal, central and western provinces is a cause for concern.[11] During 1987–98, the coastal provinces grew three percentage points more than the central regions and almost four percentage points more than the western regions. In addition, whereas in the eastern regions urban incomes are twice as high as rural incomes, in the western ones they are more than three times as high (Dahlman and Aubert, 2001). Although efforts were stepped up over the last few years and 80 million people were lifted out of poverty during 1996–2000 (over 200 million since the late 1970s), much remains to be done. Crucial to the effort of closing the gaps will be the decentralization of incentives and productive activities, and the development of agricultural and rural infrastructure.

Challenge 4: revaluing natural capital

Over 2 million people die every year in China from air and water pollution. Shifting away from resource intensive development is a high priority. In particular, the lack of water resources imposes a serious constraint. Agriculture, fisheries and ecosystems have been damaged by degraded water supplies while forests and crops suffer from acid rain from burning fossil fuels. Joint air and water pollution damages have been estimated at US$54 billion a year or 8 per cent of China's GDP in 1995 (Dahlman and Aubert, 2002).

The rapid growth of the economy has been accompanied by extensive deterioration of the environment. Indeed, if the economic impact of resource depletion is taken into account, the average annual percentage rate of growth in per capita wealth and in per capita GNP appears considerably lower than that reported through conventional national accounts (Dasgupta, 2001). Establishing a market-based pricing mechanism, adopting water conservation technologies and shifting away from resource intensive development are high on the agenda as is prevention and control of water pollution. (Chapter 5 examines the implications of WTO entry from the environmental perspective.)

Challenge 5: sustaining productivity growth

Because of resource constraints and competitive challenges, China is embarked upon the transition from a factor-based development to a productivity-driven one. It starts out far behind world leaders in technology and productivity in almost every area. Although cereal yields per hectare in China are not far from US yields, average labour productivity in agriculture is 75 per cent of India's and 0.8 per cent of those in France and the US; average labour productivity in manufacturing is 92 per cent of India's and less than 5 per cent of those of Brazil, France, Japan and the US (Dahlman and Aubert, 2002).

Labour productivity growth appears to have accelerated during the early 1990s but then slowed down across the board – though it is worth noting that both the *level* and the *rate* of growth of labour productivity in manufacturing remained far higher than in the other sectors.

China's productivity and competitiveness problem does not lie in having concentrated too much on manufacturing (all successful latecomers have). Rather, it lies in not having paid enough attention to such underpinnings of productivity growth and technical upgrading as exposure to competition and incentives to innovation and technical change (research and development (R&D), product and process improvements, efficiency gains), particularly at a time of rapid international diffusion of information and communications technologies (ICTs). The necessary development of services and intangible investment ought to be seen not as an alternative to the development of manufacturing but as a spur to its innovative drive. Large productivity differentials within the Chinese industrial economy (labour productivity is twice as high in the high technology parks as in the larger industrial sector) suggest ample scope for improved average productivity performance through domestic technology diffusion (Dahlman and Aubert, 2002).

Locally administered firms, irrespective of ownership, exhibit better productivity performance than those administered more centrally. This, in turn, suggests an important scope for regulatory and institutional reforms to improve performance. Business efficiency appears to have been considerably enhanced by shifts of administrative and regulatory responsibility to local areas (McGuckin and Dougherty, 2002).

Because of domestic social pressures, at least in the short and medium terms, China is likely to rely strongly on static comparative advantages. However, it will eventually benefit more from gains in trading efficiency from further institutional reforms and endogenous (dynamic) comparative advantages acquired through specialization and trade networking (Sachs et al., 2000). Balancing the transition towards an upgraded pattern of comparative advantages will be one of the big challenges faced by the Chinese leadership, with important implications for developing trade partners. (See Chapter 4 on the changing composition of China's exports by technology intensity and its domestic capability underpinnings.)

The focus of attention – particularly in the energy, metallurgical, chemical, machinery, automobile, building materials, construction, textile and light industries – is already on enhancing productivity, increasing product variety, improving product quality, saving on energy, reducing waste, preventing and controlling pollution. Mechanisms to support the technological renewal of key enterprises, speed up the diffusion of ICTs and domestic innovation, and foster capabilities for equipment manufacturing as well as for design and construction of complete state-of-the-art plants are also being put into place. Furthermore, large enterprises are being stimulated to strengthen their own intellectual property rights (IPRs) and competence in core products (see Chapter 7 for China's approach to IPRs). Seriously inefficient, unsafe and polluting facilities will be closed down and the necessary procedures will be adopted for financially unviable enterprises to go bankrupt.

A good deal of China's productivity gains, as well as its export growth, can be traced to foreign invested enterprises. Leading this field is non-Japanese Asian foreign direct investment (FDI), which is concentrated in labour-intensive operations: electric and electronic goods, apparel, footwear, toys, instruments and furniture (on prospects to shift this pattern towards higher technology- and skill-intensive FDI see Chapter 4). Preliminary estimates on total factor productivity (TFP) performance across provinces suggest that FDI inflows are positively associated with such performance (Graham and Wada, 2001; see also Hirschberg and Lloyd, 2000). Although much new FDI is increasingly geared to the domestic market, the positive association between FDI and productivity growth can be expected to increase, provided that a competitive environment prevails, through the introduction of state-of-the-art managerial and technological practices. These pratices can be diffused across the economy, both directly and indirectly – for instance, by stimulating SOEs' own technological and managerial updating (see below).

As in the debate on East Asian industrialization, there are conflicting views on the role of productivity growth in China's industrialization.[12] According to an estimate, TFP gains accounted for more than 42 per cent of China's growth during 1979–94 and, by the early 1990s exceeded 50 per cent, overtaking capital inputs as the most significant source of growth (Hu and Khan, 1997). Other estimates are considerably less sanguine (see, for instance Young, 2000). One point of agreement appears to be the key role played by factor reallocation relating to the introduction of profit incentives to TVEs, family farms, small private business and foreign investors and traders. As a result, the share of the state-owned sector in gross value of industrial production dramatically shrank from 78 per cent in 1979 to 26 per cent in 1999. As implied earlier on, for post-WTO entry China, the necessary shift away from resource intensive industrialization, constraints on the continuing expansion of labour-intensive activities, the need to upgrade the skill profile of the labour force and the technological and innovative performance of industry and doing away with large pockets of inefficiency, all imply a greater, not a smaller, role for productivity growth in the country's future growth. In this context, the need to enforce incentives for knowledge creation is increasingly relevant for domestic technology-based firms and industry at large (see Chapter 7).

Outward dimensions

The external risks and costs of entry

China enters the WTO in a dual role: first as a developing country; second, *vis-à-vis* some countries, notably the US, as a non-market economy. As a developing country, China has claimed certain rights, while it has voluntarily declined to exercise others (see, for instance, the case of TRIMs below). As a non-market economy, China is likely to have to endure and be involved in rough trade disputes (China is already considered the main target for anti-dumping measures in the world).[13] Box 1.1 gives a flavour of the importance of the concessions granted by China as the price of joining WTO.[14] We now focus the discussion on four particular points. First, China's commitments relating to the TRIMs agreement; second, China's commitments regarding the Technical Barriers to Trade (TBT) agreement; third, China's exposure to anti-dumping actions and product-specific safeguards that may be put forward by its major trade partners; and, fourth, exceptions requested by trade partners.

TRIMs

Complying with the WTO TRIMs agreement has been very hard for developing countries, not least those from Southeast Asia. The reason is that adhering to the agreement entailed a complete reversal of old-style, import-substitution policies that used to play a major role in

---

Box 1.1   Summary of China's key concessions

- Reduction of the average import tariff from 24.6 to 9.4 per cent
  1. From 22 to 17.5 per cent for agricultural products; elimination of subsidies for exports of agricultural exports
  2. From 25 to 8.9 per cent for industrial products*
     - From 100 to 25 per cent for vehicles and 10 per cent for vehicle parts by 2006
     - From 12.5 to 3.4 per cent (2002) and zero (2005) for information technology products
- Farm subsidies to be capped at 8.5 of production value
- Elimination of import tariffs on computers, semiconductors and other high-tech products by 2005
- Elimination of quotas by 2006
- Substantial opening of service sectors, including banking, insurance, telecommunications and professional services
  1. Up to 49 per cent foreign ownership in telecommunications and insurance after three years
  2. Importers to have own distribution networks
  3. Full market access for foreign banks within five years (currency business with local enterprises after two years)
- Broad reforms relating to transparency, notice, receptively to feed back from interested parties, uniform application of laws, judicial reviews and enforcement
- Enforcement of the stipulations of numerous WTO agreements, such as:
  1. Trade-Related Investment measures: immediate lifting of norms on local content (as of accession)
  2. Trade-Related Industrial Property Rights
  3. Technical Barriers to Trade
  4. Information Technology Agreement
- The US and other WTO members can continue considering China as 'non-market economy' for purposes of anti-dumping for 15 years
- Idem relating to product-specific safeguard mechanisms for 12 years
- A special textile safeguard allows the US to impose unilateral restrictions during 2005–8.
- Firms from WTO member countries to enjoy the same rights to trade as Chinese enterprises

- All enterprises will have the right to import and export goods and conduct trade within three years (save a few exceptions)
- Practice of two-tier pricing as well as different treatment for domestically sold and export goods to be abolished
- Remaining price controls will not aim to provide protection to domestic manufacturers and service providers
- China will be subject to a very thorough yearly oversight to monitor implementation during the first eight years, involving 21 different WTO subsidiary bodies

*By early 2001 China's average tariff for merchandise would have already been cut to 15.3 per cent, about half the level prevailing in India and roughly equivalent to tariffs in Brazil and Mexico (Lardy, 2001). Similarly, import quotas and licensing requirements, formerly pervasive, have been steadily reduced and by 2000 covered only 4 per cent of all import commodities. China's average collection rate (customs revenue divided by the total value of imports) is reported to be around 3 per cent, compared with 29 per cent for India (Goswami, 2001).

fostering industrial growth up to the very creation of the WTO (Sercovich, 1998). These include local content regulations whereby certain – often a very high percentage – of inputs and components required by foreign-controlled firms had to be purchased locally, as well as a wide range of performance requirements regarding exports, foreign exchange balances, local R&D, technology transfer, employment, etc. Automobile assembly operations were the most conspicuous target of these measures, which were justified on grounds of promoting industrialization but also for macroeconomic and balance of payment-related reasons. Indeed, some of these difficulties were anticipated in the agreement, which contained some escape clauses (ibid.). As a matter of fact, relating to the vicissitudes of the world economy since the Asian crisis of 1997–98, many developing countries did resort to such clauses, thus postponing the original deadline (1 January 2000) for a few years. Against this background, China has agreed to comply *fully* with the whole of the TRIMs agreement right *upon accession* – thus waving any grace period. This involves eliminating all foreign exchange and trade balancing, local content and export performance requirements imposed on foreign invested enterprises. The Chinese authorities pledged not to enforce the terms of contracts containing such requirements in the allocation, permission or granting of rights for importation and investment set by national or sub-national authorities. This applies to other conditions relating to R&D, provision of offsets or other forms of industrial compensation, the use of local inputs or the transfer of technology. Permission to invest or draw on import licences, quotas and tariff rate quotas are to be granted without regard to the existence of competing Chinese domestic suppliers. The industrial policy for the automotive sector will be amended correspondingly. All measures applicable to motor vehicle producers restricting the categories, types of models or vehicles permitted for production are to be completely removed two years after accession, except for the distinction between trucks and buses, light commercial vehicles and passenger cars. For motor vehicle engines the 50 per cent foreign equity limit for joint ventures was removed upon accession.[15]

These commitments set a very high bar indeed for new WTO entrants, such as Russia.

TBT

China has an important gap in the adoption of state-of-the-art quality and standards-related systems. This relates to a tradition of considering quality as an object of discretionary decisions rather than as a response to market demands. For this reason, the distinction between 'standards', which are voluntary, and 'technical regulations', which are mandatory, is often opaque. This is changing, but it will take considerable time and resources. Some WTO member countries expressed their concern that provisions for technical regulations and conformity assessment procedures do not adequately address obligations relating to transparency, non-discrimination, national treatment and avoidance of unnecessary barriers to trade. Against this backdrop, China has adopted important commitments in this field, relating to information, transparency, participation, management, adaptation and market-based mechanisms.

As from accession China has two enquiry points set up and is to publish notices of adopted and proposed technical regulations, standards and conformity assessment procedures. Private sector interests and authorities, regardless of origin, will be informed and consulted on an ongoing basis. Minimum timeframes for public comments on proposed technical regulations, standards and conformity assessment procedures will be issued. No later than four months after accession China will notify acceptance of the Code of Good Practice for the Preparation, Adoption and Application of Standards[16] and will speed up the revision of current voluntary, national, local and sectoral standards so as to harmonize them with international standards (currently some 40 per cent of the technical regulations are based on international standards; this is expected to increase by 10 per cent in five years). China will also eliminate duplicative conformity assessment procedures and impose the same requirements for imported and domestic products. China also pledged to bring the Import-Export Commodity Inspection, its implementing regulations as well as the Safety Licence System for Import Commodities into full conformity with the TBT agreement by the date of accession and not to require additional conformity assessment procedures in China for products certified by bodies recognized in China, except for random sampling of such products.

Anti-dumping and product-specific safeguards

Although the European Union (EU) and Australia no longer label China (or Russia) as a non-market economy, the US still does and will continue doing so for the next 15 years – China's right to request review under the US law of specific sectors for qualification for market economy treatment notwithstanding. Being regarded as a 'non-market economy' basically means that the prices quoted by Chinese producers/exporters may not necessarily reflect the true cost of the relevant product. As a result, when investigating dumping allegations against Chinese products, whereas the Europeans will assess them on a case-by-case basis to determine whether market conditions are met or not, the US will have the prerogative to use surrogate countries in the respective cost calculation to decide whether to levy anti-dumping charges. For instance, India's prices have been used as a benchmark of reasonable market prices, not China's, and Beijing has been unable to cite domestic costs as a defence. There have been 420 anti-dumping cases involving China in the past 20 years – 68 of them brought by the US and seven brought by China. A surge of WTO cases involving China is likely.

Is China paying a price for maintaining the peculiarities of its economic system? The answer apparently is yes and the problem is that the price to be paid is still unknown. But the risks are not one-way. A surge of trade frictions may lead to disruptions that will benefit no party, so that the stage is set for continued trade friction, particularly if China proves unable to fully implement all of its WTO obligations within the agreed time schedules.[17] Under these conditions, the US government has been advised to be 'very judicious' in applying the 'highly protectionist features' of the bilateral agreement with China (Lardy, 2001). Besides anti-dumping, under the product-specific safeguard to counter market disruption from a possible surge of imports from China, unilateral restrictions may be imposed provided that prior consultation procedures fail. This provision will apply for 12 years after China's WTO entry. These measures have never before applied to any General Agreement on Tariff and Trade (GATT)/WTO applicants (ibid.) and might constrain China's ability to increase world export market shares.

Exceptions

A number of WTO member countries have left notice of prohibitions, quantitative restrictions and other measures against imports from China that they intend to apply in a manner inconsistent with the WTO agreement. These measures are to be phased out in accordance with mutually agreed terms and timetable. The countries concerned are Argentina, the European Communities, Hungary, Mexico and the Slovak Republic. Let us illustrate three of these cases.

Mexico, by far the most important case of this kind, will apply anti-dumping measures for six years, without progressive phasing out, against a wide range of products covering 1310 tariff lines.[18] The key product clusters involved are: clothing (415 tariff lines), textiles (403), organic chemicals (258), electric machines, appliances and equipment (78), footwear (56), tools (48) and toys (21).

Argentine measures consist of specific duties on textiles and clothing, non-sporting footwear and toys for five years. Duties in excess of 35 per cent will be phased out progressively, after which a 35 per cent *ad valorem* duty will remain.

In the case of the European Communities the measures consist of quotas on footwear and porcelain and ceramic tableware and kitchenware to be progressively eliminated within five years.

Major challenges for developing Asia

Because of its low labour costs, growing availability of skilled manpower, very large market and attractive business climate, China is a magnet for FDI, including that consisting of reallocation of production capacity from other places in the region (particularly Taiwan Province and Hong Kong SAR). Much of the outsourcing to the Southeast Asian countries that took place during the 1980s and 1990s is now being shifted to China. This will accelerate as a result of WTO accession.[19]

Largely because of factor cost advantages, China's world market shares are expected to go up by about 50 per cent in 2002 as compared with 1995, with the breakdown shown in Table 1.1.

Table 1.1 Projection of China's share in global exports in selected sectors (in percentages)

Product	1995	2005
Textiles	8.4	10.6
Apparel	20.0	47.0
Metals	3.4	6.5
Autos	0.1	2.2
Electronics	5.0	9.8
Total (average)	3.7	6.8

Source: Booth (2002).

Wages in China are 20 per cent lower than in the Philippines, one-third of Malaysia's and one-quarter of Thailand's. China's labour costs may become the benchmark for labour costs across the region and beyond. At the same time, China turns out nearly 30 times as many engineering graduates every year as Thailand and almost 2.5 times as many as Japan (Supachai and Clifford, 2002, Chapter 4; see also Chapter 4 of this book).

Countries such as Vietnam and Pakistan are among the few that will remain competitive in labour-intensive activities. On the other end, countries such as the Republic of Korea, Taiwan Province of China and Japan will also hold their competitive position in high-quality products.

The trade creation derived from entry-related developments will favour the relatively more developed AP countries due to China's need to substantially expand imports of medium and high technology goods (for a breakdown of trade impact by sub-region and *vis-à-vis* third markets, see Chapter 3). As China itself is becoming a sizeable exporter of this kind of goods, two-way trade with those countries can also be expected to grow rapidly.[20]

AP countries in between the most and the least advanced of the region, such as Malaysia, the Philippines, Thailand, will face the most difficulties. Although fully aware of the dimension of the challenge ahead of them, these Southeast Asian countries are not necessarily ready to take bold steps. The weaknesses of their industrialization pattern, especially in terms of entrepreneurship and technological mastery, are being exposed. Some countries, for example Thailand, are already poised to prevent substantial losses in competitive standing by restructuring industry while others, such as Malaysia, expect to get into reciprocal FDI operations with China.[21] However, domestic concerns have been getting in the way of the required acceleration in regional economic integration, particularly in automobiles. The Southeast Asian countries that rely heavily on labour-intensive exports such as textiles, clothing and electronics, but cannot match China's labour costs (Philippines, Malaysia, Indonesia), may suffer market and employment losses unless offset by proactive responses.[22] The relatively more advanced AP developing countries, although in a different predicament, also need to react swiftly.[23] For them it is essential to take bold steps towards intensified intra-industry specialization and two-way trade with China as well as expanding reciprocal FDI. Countries such as Taiwan Province of China and Singapore, which have been losing considerable market share to China in high-technology goods and/or reallocating much of their capacity to China have, in addition, little choice but to go upstream in the value chain.

Over 60 per cent of China-bound FDI goes into manufacturing. Vast availability of increasingly skilled labour, in addition to a substantially improved infrastructure and freer trade, guarantee a substantial expansion of its ever more technology-intensive manufacturing capabilities before the cost of manpower starts rising significantly. Assembly businesses are enticing their parts and component suppliers to set up shop in China, with cost savings of up to one-third. Tariff cuts on inputs and low taxes (even after the lifting of preferences applied to the investment zones) as well as the relaxation of restrictions on trading and distribution rights help to reduce costs. Indeed, these cost cuts and increased competition are causing a considerable compression of profit margins. And falling prices, already observable not just in automobiles, but also in home appliances, are likely to affect margins in the whole region – and will entice further reallocation moves to China and exert pressure on exchange rates. It is conjectured that the combination of low wages and global trade deflation may cause the greatest reallocation of capital ever seen and make China the world's dominant manufacturer within a decade (EUI, 2002).

China is expected to start buying foreign companies and research laboratories to acquire foreign knowledge as did Japan, Republic of Korea and Taiwan Province of China in the past – one of the keys to their technological catching up. In the long run, as labour costs progressively rise in China, it will rely less and less on relatively low-skill exports, and thus leave more room for those countries that come behind.

Spillovers from China entry

A number of externalities will derive from China's accession to the WTO. Let us single out four of them.

- The terms of admission will serve as a model for a number of other transition economies that are seeking WTO membership, notably Russia. The requisites for entry have been set considerably higher than so far.
- WTO's dispute settlement capacity may be overwhelmed by trade conflicts involving China. The largest trading partners will share the responsibility of seeking effective ways to prevent paralysis.
- China's entry at a time of a new round centred on development may catalyze adjustments in the informal governance structure of the WTO towards some strengthening of the role of developing countries in agenda setting (see Chapter 6 on the implications of China's entry from the developing country's standpoint).
- China may displace some apparel exports from other countries, particularly to the US market, as a result of the liberalization of textile and apparel trade and Permanent Normal Trade Relations (PNTR) while, as an emerging high-technology powerhouse, China will present a growing challenge to other AP countries that also export high-technology goods

The genie is out of the bottle. There is no way back now. In the last resort, the outcome will depend on the commitment, good judgement and good will of all key parties concerned.

This book closes with a timely set of reflections by Supachai Panitchpakdi (Chapter 8), who provides an overview of new challenges for sustainable industrial development in a world of rapid technological change, globalization and an international trading system organized around the WTO agreements and a final summary chapter by Long Yongtu and Carlos Magariños.

Endnote

On market socialism

The concept of a 'socialist market economic system' is not easily grasped in the West. This is only to be expected, since the Chinese are building such a system largely as they go, by dismantling the command economy and letting the terms of an increasing number of transactions in the commodity, labour and capital markets be determined by market forces (see Box 1.2). Most prices are already determined by demand and supply, not by government decree, and more than 70 per cent of the industrial output value is produced by the non-state sector.

Box 1.2   China's socialist market economy: sequence of landmark decisions and expected achievements

- 1978: The CPC's 11th Central Committee shifts policy stress to socialist modernization and reform and opening to the outside world (remuneration is linked to output; integration of centralization and decentralization through a two-layer management system is introduced; control on prices of most agricultural products is relaxed; the industrial structure in rural areas is adjusted through the creation of township enterprises)
- 1984: The CPC's 12th Central Committee decides on the restructuring of the economic system to an urban centred stage
- 1992: The CPC's 14th National Congress establishes Deng Xiaoping's theory of building socialism with Chinese characteristics as guiding policy and puts forward economic reform towards a socialist market economic system (macro-adjustment and control measures are adopted; public ownership continues being the main form of ownership, but various other types of ownership are developed; SOEs are to be further transformed to meet the requirements of the market economy; property rights and responsibilities of enterprises to be clearly defined, their functions to be separated from those of the government and scientifically managed; the national market system to be unified, integrating urban and rural markets; establishment of an income distribution system according to work where precedence is given to efficiency and fairness in distribution is taken into account; a multi-tier social security system to be set up
- 1997: The CPC's 15th National Congress regards the non-public ownership sector an important part of China's socialist economy; key production factors, such as capital and technology, as entitled to participate in income distribution
- 1999: Substantial progress made in areas such as the liberalization of the grain market and SOEs and banking system reform. New proposals are put forward to reform the housing and medical insurance systems and plans for the reform of the investment, banking, financial and taxation systems are formulated. The functions of the market in resources allocation are strengthened
- 2001: Private entrepreneurs are allowed to join the CPC
- 2010: Achievement of a sound socialist market economy
- 2020: Achievement of a mature socialist market economy

However, in contrast with other transition economies, the Chinese do not view this process as one of introducing 'best practice' capitalist institutions. The idea, as put forward by Deng Xiaoping at the 14th National Congress of the Chinese Communist Party (CPC) held in 1992, is 'building socialism with Chinese characteristics as the guiding policy in China'.

Stiglitz (1996) questioned market socialism as depicted by Lange and Lerner in the 1930s (Lange, 1938; Lerner, 1938) as seriously flawed because it is founded, as is neoclassical economics, on the first and second fundamental theorems of welfare economics, that is, on the assumption of general economic equilibrium with a complete set of perfectly competitive markets. Stiglitz holds that, in a world of imperfect information, convexities and externalities, a constraint Pareto optimum can never be reached. However, government intervention may *potentially* create Pareto improvements in the economy.

The Chinese approach would appear to be in line with these views, for instance in thinking that subjecting firms to real competition is more important than changing ownership. The distinction between market capitalism and market socialism is largely about the appropriate balance between markets and government, rather than, as in old-fashion socialism, replacing one with the other. It is about having the visible hand of the state, rather then the invisible hand of the markets, as the ultimate judge, based on the potential efficiency-enhancing properties of the state on grounds, for instance, of the theorems of the new information-theoretic economics. Furthermore, Stiglitz posits that there is no intellectual foundation for the separation of efficiency and equity concerns. Although this is no doubt built into the current Chinese approach, this approach does appear to prioritize efficiency over old-fashioned socialist equality: 'an income distribution system based on distribution according to work will be established in which *efficiency is given precedence and fairness in distribution is taken into account'* (italics added) (see www.china.org.cn/ e-china/economicre-structuring.htm). Still, the Chinese seem to adopt important elements of the Lange–Lerner–Taylor approach (Lange, 1938; Lerner, 1938; Taylor, 1929), that is, if SOE managers enjoy enough independence in business decisions, the efficiency of the free market can be reproduced without private property. Indeed, the Chinese authorities are taking bold steps to strengthen leadership groups in vital, backbone SOEs (Wei, 2002). Note, however, that the CPC has recently committed the country to a massive privatization programme of all but the largest 300 or so SOEs (Ramanujan, 2001).

Notes

1 The WTO, based in Geneva, Switzerland, was created in 1995. It is the successor of the General Agreement on Tariffs and Trade (GATT), which provided the rules for the world trading system. Whereas GATT mainly dealt with trade in goods, the WTO and its agreements cover trade in services, intellectual property rights (IPRs), trade-related investment measures (TRIMs), technical barriers to trade (TBT) and other areas. The WTO is the only international body dealing with the rules of trade between nations. The WTO has a mechanism for the impartial settlement of trade disputes among its members to assist ensuring progress in trade liberalization through negotiation. WTO's fundamental principles include non-discrimination, national treatment, reciprocity and transparency. See http://www.wto.org. For the English version of the documents relating to China's accession to the WTO see http://www.moftec.gov.cn.

2 On market socialism see endnote to this chapter.

3 China pioneered the development of mechanized industry and empirical research of natural phenomena. In terms of sheer economic strength, it remained at the world frontier until the eighteenth century (at that time India occupied the second place). But well before then it cut itself off new breakthroughs, notably those of the industrial revolution. Were it not because of this, China might well still be the world's leading economy. Now China is ready to try again, catch up and forge ahead. However, sight should not be lost of the fact that, although it has been catching up at a very accelerated pace since the late 1970s, China still has a long way to go – although not that long, according to some estimates (Maddison, 1998). By 2010 China expects to have a 400–500 million large middle-income population, which would make its domestic market larger than that of the US.

4 In the short run, this risk is greater for developing than for the developed countries; however, this need not be the case in the medium and long run (see below).

5 Just as with legal expertise, China will also have heavy incremental demand for expertise in the fields of anti-dumping, anti-subsidies, countervailing and safeguard measures, TBT and IPRs.

6 Imports of some items, such as autos, steel and some farm produce have started to climb and firms began to get embroiled in price wars or in competition with cheaper imports just after tariffs came down on 1 January 2002 in line with WTO commitments. An early signal of the perils faced by Chinese SOEs, not just in heavy, but also in light industry, is that of Jianlibao, the apparently well-established soft-drink producer, which owns some of the best-known brands in China. Unable to face the competition of multinational firms (its share of the carbonated-drinks market has slipped from around 15 per cent to less than 5 per cent), it has recently become a target for takeover.

7 China has 21 million TVEs employing 128 million rural residents and generating combined exports of US$115 billion. TVEs have become a key force driving China's market economy since their creation 40 years ago and are getting involved in farm product processing, textiles and household electrical appliances (Huanxin, 2002).

8 On policy reform for developing countries in general, with emphasis on ensuring sustainable productivity growth, see Magariños and Sercovich (eds) (2001).

9 Non-performing loans held by Chinese banks would amount to US$218 billion, or 27 per cent of total bank lending. Non-official estimates regard that figure as twice as high (Chandler, 2002).

10 China's current problems are best captured in the outline of the tenth FYP for national economic and social development submitted by Premier Zhu Rongji on occasion of the Fourth Session of the Ninth National People's Congress (NPC). He pointed out that the principal problems still to be addressed included inappropriate industrial structure and non-coordinated development of local economies, low overall quality of the national economy and low competitiveness in the international market; imperfections in the socialist market economy and conspicuous systematic factors hampering the development of productive forces; a comparative backward state of science, technology and education and relatively weak innovative ability in science and technology; a shortage of important resources, such as water and petroleum, and the deterioration of the ecological environment in some regions; growing unemployment pressure, slow income increase of farmers and some urban residents, and an increasing income gap; considerable disorder in some areas of the market economy; frequent occurrences of grave accidents; serious corruption, extravagance and waste, formalism and bureaucracy; and poor public order in some localities. See http://www.china.org.cn/english/8449.htm.

11 There is some debate about how serious this problem is. For instance, Qian argues that observers' common emphasis on regional unevenness consists, for the most part, in an exaggeration of the role of exogenous factors (particularly FDI) in accounting for China's growth, since FDI has been heavily concentrated in the coastal provinces (Qian, 2001) whereas, actually, that growth would have been not just a phenomenon of the coastal provinces but across-the-board, both coastal and inland. In fact, official statistics report a rather unchanged balance among the coastal, central and western regions during the past 20 years in population, employment and output. However, this appears to be largely due to a reporting distortion: much labour force attracted to the coastal provinces remains registered in the provinces of origin.

12 On the macro and micro dimensions of productivity growth in international perspective, see Sercovich (1999, ch. 6).

13 China and Japan have already agreed to set up a bilateral mechanism to prevent future trade frictions, along the lines of the one that Japan has with the US.

14 'Beijing has committed to tariff rates that are lower than any other developing country, and it has foregone the use of key subsidies that the WTO normally permits. It has allowed other governments to shut out its goods with much less justification than required under existing international trade law and permitted them to retain import restrictions on textile and clothing products for an unusually long time,' Garten (2001).

15 See World Trade Organization (2001).

16   For details on this Code see http://www.iso.ch/iso/en/comms-markets/wto/pdf/tbt-a3.pdf.

17   So far, however, China has been running ahead of schedule, for instance, in connection with foreign shareholding in broadband telecommunications services and tariff reductions on items covered by the Information Technology Agreement (ITA). Likewise, a number of important domestic laws covering patents, copyrights, trademarks and foreign investment have already been amended.

18   Originally Mexico sought to apply these measures for 15 years, while China offered five years (Spagat, 2001).

19   An additional advantage, this time in the making, is the setting up of China's Export Credit Insurance Corporation (Sinosure), the first specialized export insurance agency in China, which aims to build itself into a world-class export credit provider within the next five years. Sinosure will focus its business on the export of high technology and high value-added electronic products, the fastest growing in Chinese exports (see Chapter 4).

20   Premier Zhu Rongji has proposed a substantial expansion of intra-industry trade and reciprocal FDI in information technology and electronic goods between China and India relying on their competitive strengths in hardware and software, respectively. In consumer electronics he quoted China as offering prices six times lower than India (Dow Jones, 2002).

21   Proton, the Malaysian car maker is already considering investing in car-parts manufacturing in China.

22   In fact, several members of the Association of Southeast Asian Nations (ASEAN) are reported to have launched innovative initiatives, such as fuel and medicinal applications from palm oil (Malaysia) and organic agricultural products (the Philippines), in this case to compete with Chinese food exports, which raise concerns about contamination by pesticides and pollution. This goes along with moves towards closer trade cooperation with China.

23   Increased actual and potential competition is already prompting moves in Asia to invest more in R&D, branding and labelling. For instance, on grounds of competition from China in steel, shipbuilding and consumer electronics, the government of the Republic of South Korea has earmarked around US$7.7 billion to foster the development of knowledge-based industries, including bioengineering, environment, information and nanotechnologies (Booth, 2002). China itself is taking steps in a similar direction. Vice-Minister Sun Zhenyu (MOFTEC) recently announced the decision to support the development of high-technology exports in the fields of information technology, biotechnology and medicine, new materials, consumer electronics and home appliances. One hundred exporting enterprises and 92 exported products have been earmarked for support to ensure a 15 per cent annual growth in exports over the next five years (Dow Jones, 2001). Meanwhile, multinational corporations (MNCs) are taking steps towards their own regional division of labour. For instance, Matsushita Electric (Japan) is restructuring its operations to fully combine Taiwan's technological research potential with China's mass production capacity. Matsushita China is also consolidating its 40 production bases scattered across China (Guan, 2002). Along with Hitachi, Toshiba and

Acer, Samsung, is reported to be closing down domestic or Asia-based factories and moving them to China.

References and bibliography

Booth, J. (2002), 'A new era: China joins the WTO – Asian business feel heat from neighbors', *Asian Wall Street Journal*, 15 January.

Chandler, C. (2002), 'Trying to make good on bad debt reform – China selling bank assets to solve problem', *The Washington Post*, 15 January.

Dahlman, C. J. and Aubert, J.-E. (2001), *China and the Knowledge Economy*, WBI Development Studies (Washington DC: World Bank).

Dasgupta, P. (2001), 'Valuing objects and evaluating policies in imperfect economies', Presidential Address, Annual Conference of the Royal Economic Society, University of St Andrews, July.

Dow Jones International News (2001), 'China plans to continue subsidies for companies post-WTO', 16 November 2001.

—— (2002), 'China and India should be economic partners, not rivals – Zhu Rongji', 16 January.

EUI (2002), 'China industry – manufacturing market has it made', Country Briefing, Economics Intelligence Unit, 22 January.

Garten, J. E. (2001), 'China in the WTO: let's cut it some slack', *Businessweek*, 8 October.

Goswami, O. (2001), 'China and the WTO', *Business Standard* (New Delhi, 3 February 2001).

Graham, E. M. and Wada, E. (2001), 'Foreign direct investment in China: effects on growth and economic performance', Institute for International Economics (Washington DC).

Guan, E. (2002), 'Matsushita Taiwan set to be squeezed by Matsushita China', *Taiwan Business News*, 18 January.

Hirschberg, J. G. and Lloyd, P. J. (2000), 'An application of pot-dea boots trap regression analysis to the spill over of the technology and foreign-invested enterprises in China', Department of Economics, University of Melbourne, January.

Hu, Z. and Khan, M. S. (1997), 'Why is China growing so fast?', Working Paper 96/75, International Monetary Fund (Washington DC: June).

Huanxin, Z. (2002), 'WTO entry to help township firms grow', *China Daily*, 21 January.

Lange, O. (1938), *On the Economic Theory of Socialism* (Minnesota: University of Minnesota Press).

Lardy, N. R. (2001), 'China economic brief issues for the new administration and Congress', CSIS (Washington, DC, March 2001).

Lerner, A. P. (1938), 'Theory and practice of socialist economics', *Review of Economic Studies*, 6, 71–5.

Luppincott, B. S. (ed) (1956), *On the Economic Theory of Socialism* (New York: McGraw-Hill).

Maddison, A. (1998), *Chinese Economic Performance in the Long Run*, Development Centre Studies (Paris: OECD, 1998).

Magariños, C.A. and Sercovich, F.C. (eds) (2001), *Gearing up for a New Development Agenda – Marginalization vs Prosperity: How to Improve and Spread the Gains of Globalization* (Vienna: UNIDO, 2001).

McGuckin, R. H. and Dougherty, S. M. (2002), *Restructuring Chinese Enterprises: the Effects of Federalism and Privatization Initiatives on Business Performance*, Research Report R-1311-02-RR, The Conference Board (New York).

Qian, Y. (2001), 'How reform worked in China', draft, Department of Economics (University of California, Berkeley).

Ramanujan, T. C. A. (2001), 'Decisive steps in disinvestment', *Business Line*, Madras, 19 December.

Sachs, J., Yang, X. and Zhang, D. (2000), 'Globalization, dual economy and economic development', *China Economic Review* 11 (2000), 189–209.

Sercovich, F. (1998), 'Best practices, policy convergence and the WTO Trade-Related Investment Measures Agreement', *ECLAC Review,* 64, LCG 2022 (Santiago, April).

Sercovich, F. et al. (1999), 'Competition and the world economy – comparing industrial development policies in the developing and transition economies', Edward Elgar and UNIDO (Cheltenham, UK: Edward Elgar and Northampton, MA: UNIDO).

Spagat, E. (2001), 'China WTO entry sparks fear in Mexico factories', Dow Jones Newswires, 5 February 2001.

Stiglitz, J. (1996), *Whither Socialism?* (Cambridge, MA: MIT Press, 1996).

Supachai, P. and Clifford M. L. (2002), *China and the WTO – Changing China, Changing WTO* (Singapore: John Wiley and Sons (Asia)).

Taylor, F. M. (1929), 'The guidance of production in a socialist state', *American Economic Review,* 19 (1), reprinted in Luppincott 1956.

World Trade Organization (2001), *Report of the Working Party on the Accession of China*, WT/ACC/CHN/49, 1 October.

Wei, Z. (2202), 'SOE leadership groups to be strengthened' (Xinhua: New China's News Agency, 22 January).

Young, A. (2000), 'Gold into base metals: productivity growth in the People's Republic of China during the reform period', Working Paper 7856, National Bureau of Economic Research (Cambridge, MA, August 2002) http://www.nber.org/papers/w7856.

2
Negotiating Entry: Key Lessons Learned

Long Yongtu

(China) P33 O19
F13 F14

China's accession to the World Trade Organization (WTO) has taken 15 years of arduous and protracted negotiations. Assessing this process is a worthy undertaking, albeit one that invites controversy. Many thought that, as a major trading country, China was to join the WTO as a matter of course. Others thought that, because of its sheer size and importance, the WTO had to handle China's accession with the utmost care. Whichever the approach, 15 years of negotiations seem far too long to achieve such a goal, particularly in relation to the average time taken by others who have acceded to the WTO.

Oddly enough, as the chief negotiator, having had to endure so many difficulties and shoulder so many burdens along this long process, I now believe that it may prove to be a good thing for China to have undergone these difficult years of negotiation. It may seem illogical, but it is true. The key is how one views the accession process. If you look at this process of negotiation only as one in which you have to make endless concessions to your partners and confront endless challenges at home for the sake of obtaining a WTO membership card, then you would find this process very painful and long indeed. If, instead, you look at the process from a strategic point of view, in the framework of China's long-term economic development as well as its relationships with the rest of the world, you will find that many positive elements have been generated through this historic process.

Building a consensus

The fact is that many people only perceive the apparent toughness and painfulness of the negotiations themselves. They do not know that there is another side to the coin, an even tougher and therefore more significant process: one of consensus-building among our own people at home on some major issues which are confronted not only by China but also by many other countries, especially the developing ones.

The issues include, although are not limited to:

- How economic globalization should be addressed
- How to achieve a balance between trade liberalization and the promotion of development
- How to tackle social issues such as unemployment in the restructuring of the economy

It is the process of consensus-building around these major issues at home which turns out to be the most important component of China's WTO negotiations.

The fact that China's accession to an international organization would have such a wide impact throughout the world is something we had not expected at all. The important thing is that we in China have successfully and skilfully handled the domestic side of the accession process and have transformed the pressure generated by these negotiations, both at home and abroad, and turned them into a promoter, a catalyst for China's historic process of economic reform and opening to the outside world – a process started by Deng Xiaoping 23 years ago.

That is the most significant lesson we can draw from the negotiations: that we have involved not only dozens of negotiators but also millions of ordinary Chinese in the process. To some extent, the process became an unprecedented, massive education programme for our people regarding globalization and the restructuring of the economy, with their positive as well as negative implications for their day-to-day life. I believe that this striking feature of China's WTO accession, not as a diplomatic exercise in Geneva but as a range of broad-based activities involving millions of people in a quest for a better life, is a unique experience in the modern world.

The issues China had to confront

In order to understand this unique feature of China's accession to the WTO, it is important to examine the major outcomes of the past 15 years of negotiation. In order to acquire the right to WTO membership, China has made numerous commitments, which can be grouped in two broad categories: first, to observe international rules and practices;

and second, to gradually open up its market. By committing itself to international rules and practices, China is addressing some of the fundamental problems it has faced in the economic reform and opening-up process.

Firstly, the market economy China is determined to create should be based on the rule of law. A sense of rules has certainly been lacking in China. The planned economy it had pursued for several decades was based on the rules of men, and to make matters more complicated, several thousand years of feudal society had given the 'rule of men' deep roots. So China's economic reform has reached a critical stage, namely that of making the rule of law an essential element in its economic system. It is against this background that China's commitment to international rules and practices arising from the WTO accession negotiations has become an integral feature of its economic reform process.

As China has committed itself to making its domestic laws and regulations consistent with WTO rules, it has had to start an extensive clean-up of its existing legal system. This 'clean-up' includes the massive task of repealing or modifying numerous laws and regulations. According to information provided by the Legal Office of the Central Government (State Council), since the year 2000, 30 ministries have cleaned up 2300 laws and regulations, decided to repeal 830 and proposed amendments to 325.

The National People's Congress, China's legislative body, completed in July 2001 the revisions of the Law on Chinese Foreign Cooperative Enterprises, Law on Foreign Capital Enterprises, Customs Law, Patents Law, Trademarks Law and Copyright Law. The revision of these laws has aimed at making them fully compliant with WTO rules, mainly those embodied in the Trade-Related Investment Measures (TRIMs) and Trade-Related Industrial Property (TRIP) Agreements. These revisions have made illegal such practices as government imposition on foreign capital enterprises of compulsory requirements of local content, foreign exchange balances, export performance, and local procurement – which are not permitted under the provisions of TRIMs.

At the same time, China is also prepared to establish reasonable legal measures to protect domestic industries and the domestic market in those situations where WTO rules allow them, under the so-called 'Safety Valve' mechanism (which must be set up concurrently with the lowering of tariffs and opening of the market, once China is in the WTO). These measures include, among others, modifying and drafting anti-dumping regulations, anti-subsidy regulations and special safeguards.

In accordance with its commitment to the transparency of laws and regulations, the Chinese government has established an enquiry point within the Ministry of Foreign Trade and Economic Cooperation (MOFTEC) to provide legal information to the public and clarify legal rules.

As legal reforms have accelerated hand-in-hand with accession to the WTO, China's economic reform process has entered a new stage hallmarked by emphasis on the rule of law and the importance of making laws consistent with international practice. This progress in the legal aspect has certainly had far-reaching impact on China's economic reforms, giving them greater sustainability and international recognition.

Secondly, after 20 years of reform and market opening, as tremendous progress has been achieved in economic development and improvement of people's livelihoods, China has also witnessed the emergence of serious market disorders, including smuggling, corruption, bribery, sham goods, tax evasion, counterfeit goods and pirated software. These have become the tumur in the body of China's economy. The Chinese government is launching an extensive campaign against those evils in the market, fully aware of the long-term significance of this action. WTO accession, including the enforcement of international rules, has certainly given the government the full legitimacy to take strong, sweeping measures to deal with these issues.

The government realizes that it is dealing not only with an imminent threat to the establishment of a true market economy; it is also addressing some fundamental obstacles to creating a society based on values of reliability, honesty and truthfulness. Business practices and public management are not just a set of rules; they also are a state of mind. Therefore, upon having completed the accession negotiations, an unprecedented extensive training programme has been set up for the whole country on WTO rules, additionally thought of as a driver to forge the ethical values of honesty and trustworthiness, both in business practices and in people's daily lives. This educational programme, which is partly a result of the WTO accession, will change not only the business environment but, more importantly, the social and ethical environment of the Chinese people in the twenty-first century.

Thirdly, in its opening-up to the outside world, one of China's key achievements is that of having become the premier location for foreign direct investment (FDI) among the developing countries, with a yearly average of US$40 billion in the last decade.

FDI today plays an important role in China's economic development, contributing 50 per cent of its imports and exports, 20 per cent of its tax revenue, 30 per cent of its industrial output and, more importantly, generating more than 20 million jobs every year. It is of paramount importance to keep up the volume of FDI and improve the quality of the investment. In spite of all the efforts already made by the government, including an array of preferential treatments, there is still much room for improvement in China's investment environment. The chief complaint that an increasing number of foreign investors and business people are making to the government now is the lack of a transparent, predictable and stable legal environment.

In China, there are numerous so-called 'internal regulations' governing business practices. These were only known to a few people, a situation which conspired against the desired transparency of law. In many cases the local regulations were not consistent with national rules, even less with international practices, and they were changing all the time, making predictability almost impossible. As a result, the investment environment has been deteriorating in some parts of China, where the government must take decisive action to stop random fees and fines, compulsory donations and unauthorized inspections of the foreign capital enterprises. In this connection, China's WTO accession has provided timely recipes to improve the business environment for FDI flows.

Improving the environment for FDI

The 'recipe' subscribed by China's WTO accession has been clearly stipulated in provisions of the protocol of the accession, which include:

Transparency

This is crucial to ensure certainty for business. Since our experience proves that foreign investors do not have to like everything in the legal regime, the important thing is for them to know as much as possible about the laws, regulations and other elements of the operating environment. In view of the specific conditions of China, the protocol provides that:

- China undertakes to enforce only those laws, regulations and other measures that are published and readily available to other WTO members

- China shall establish or designate an official journal for the publication of all laws, regulations and other measures, and provide a reasonable period for comment before such measures are implemented (except those involving national security and those whose publication would impede law enforcement)
- China shall establish a designated enquiry point to provide timely information on relevant laws and regulations

Independent judicial review

Our experience also proves that a transparent legal framework should entail equal access to the law for companies in their commercial actions. These actions should not just be ones between companies, but also actions by companies against government. In this connection, the protocol states:

- China should establish or designate, and maintain, tribunals and contact points for the prompt review of all administrative actions relating to the implementation of laws. Such tribunals should be impartial and independent of the agencies entrusted with administrative enforcement
- If the initial right of appeal is to an administrative body, there should always be the opportunity to choose to appeal the decision to a judicial body

Uniform application

As the implementation of national laws by the national government has been one of the pressing concerns of foreign investors, China has committed itself in the protocol to a special section on 'uniform application'. This is not only important to eliminate conflicts between local regulations and national laws but also essential to root out all kinds of local protectionism at various levels. The section provides:

- China should apply and administer all its laws, regulations and other measures of the central government as well as the local ones in a uniform, impartial and reasonable manner
- China's local regulations, rules and other measures shall conform to the obligations undertaken in the WTO Agreement and the accession protocol

In summary, China's WTO commitment to observe international rules will help China to build a market economy based on the rule of law, a market economy with order, and a market economy with a transparent, stable and predicable legal environment. All these are not only fundamental for China to move into a truly market-driven economic system, but also important for China to maintain the reputation of the Chinese business environment in order to attract more FDI and to avoid unnecessary trade disputes with its fellow WTO members.

A two-way process

By committing itself to a gradually more open market, China has highlighted some important points.

In the first place, China believes that market opening is a two-way process. China, as an increasingly important trading country in the world, cannot just take advantage of the markets of others; it has to open its own market. This is the principle of mutual benefit and no-discrimination. It is also of fundamental importance to reduce trade frictions and disputes.

However, China has forcefully held that the opening of the domestic market, especially by developing countries, should be a gradual process. The extent of opening should be in line with the level of development of the individual countries concerned. That is why China insisted very firmly on its developing-country status during the whole period of negotiations. China has successfully convinced its negotiation partners that market opening is not an objective by itself.

Market opening should be at the service of market growth and be conducive to domestic economic development. Otherwise, it would only lead to a situation, where, as the Chinese proverb goes, 'One kills the hen in order to get the egg.' It would be a real tragedy for trade negotiators if, after such tough negotiations, they find that the 'market' has been opened but that, actually, the market has ceased to exist because there is no economic growth and residents have no purchasing power.

Since China and its negotiation partners, especially those from developed world, have come to a common understanding that only a gradual opening of Chinese market can bring a win-win outcome for all parties concerned, some 'red lines' imposed by the Chinese side have not been crossed in the negotiations:

- In financial services, the capital market in local currency will not be opened to foreign competition

- In telecommunications and life insurance, only 50 per cent foreign ownership is allowed. Management control by the foreign partners is excluded
- In agriculture, China should be entitled to grant a higher level of subsidies as compared to developed countries (8.5 per cent *vis-à-vis* 5 per cent ceiling for the latter)

In addition to the above, many arrangements for the transitional period have been stipulated to ensure a gradual opening. Here are some examples:

- In telecommunications, geographic restrictions on paging and value-added services will be phased out two years after WTO accession, while the phasing-out period for mobile and domestic fixed line services will be five and six years, respectively
- In banking, foreign banks will be allowed to conduct local currency business with Chinese enterprises two years after entering, and with individual Chinese citizens after five years

We believe that these outcomes have taken into account the level of maturity reached in each and every sector under negotiation. Therefore, these arrangements will not jeopardize the development of these industries; on the contrary, they will promote their development by means of healthy and appropriate competition from outside.

Secondly, China believes that the main benefit of opening up to trade and investment flows is to catalyze change in Chinese domestic industries, not just to generate foreign currency. China is not opening itself up so that foreign products can flood China's market; it is opening the market to enhance the competitiveness of Chinese industries.

Of all the sectors opening up to competition after China's WTO accession, for many people agriculture would be the most vulnerable, and therefore the most exposed to massive import competition – since, with WTO entry, China's average tariff on agriculture imports will fall to 15 per cent from 22 per cent in trade-weighted terms, affecting mainly wheat, maize, rice and vegetable oil. At face value, this may be true. However, it is believed that China's entry provides a real opportunity to restructure its agricultural sector, which has been the least opened and lags relatively behind other industries in the reform process.

Compared with advanced countries, China's agriculture does not enjoy comparative advantage in producing some foodstuffs from wheat, corn, soybeans and other vegetable oil crops. China has only 7 per cent of the world's arable land, but has to feed 20 per cent of the world's population. In addition, many areas of China are short of water supply. Therefore, as some agricultural experts argue, China should import more grain, as this is tantamount to the import of scarce land and water resources. Given China's dimensions, even if it imports the full tariff-quota volume of grains (about 22 million tons a year), such imports would still amount to less than 5 per cent of its total production of these crops. This means that food security could be guaranteed, even in the very unlikely event of a 'food embargo'. Therefore China should be resolute in restructuring its agriculture sector so as to move to its more competitive areas, such as fruits, vegetables and meat – as WTO membership will bring greater access to foreign markets.

In any event, WTO entry will certainly exert a major influence on the government to introduce a more rational and fair policy towards agriculture, strengthening it with better infrastructure and services, and by alleviating the financial burden and increasing the incomes of the farmers.

The development of the agricultural sector after WTO accession could prove that WTO entry was a turning point for China's agricultural policy and the driving force behind a new phase, seeking to achieve world standards of competitiveness. China believes that another key benefit of opening up to world trade and investment flows is the cultivation of new industries in order to generate massive employment, which is critical for China's sustainable economic development as well as social stability.

As a result of the WTO market-access negotiation, China has made the most significant offer of opening up in the service sector. The service sector is relatively undeveloped in China, accounting for only 35 per cent of its gross domestic product (GDP) – a lower ratio than in some developing countries and even more so with respect to the developed countries, where the service sector accounts for 65–85 per cent of GDP. Still more remarkable from the Chinese government's standpoint is that the service sector has a weight in terms of employment in those countries which is similar to its weight in their GDP. In consequence, the Chinese government is determined to restructure the economy and make special efforts to develop its service industries. Its experience in developing some of its most advanced manufacturing sectors, such as electronic home appliances, has led the government to believe that the Chinese service sector will also follow the same road by opening up to foreign competition.

This is the reason why so many major market openings will take place in banking, insurance, telecommunications, distribution, tourism, transportation and professional services. We believe that the opening -up of these service sectors will generate mass job opportunities, especially middle- and high-income jobs, which is important to ensure work prospects at home for the talented young Chinese rather than compelling them to seek jobs abroad. The paramount consideration of creating more jobs is not only reflected in opening up the service sector, but also in some of the major manufacturing sectors.

The automobile industry is a typical case. The long-time protection of the auto industry has made it inefficient and uncompetitive, and has made cars, both imported and domestically produced, so highly priced that they were out of reach of the bulk of the population. This has prevented the expansion of the domestic market.

This is why for so many years private car sales increased very slowly in China. Even more worrying is that all the service providers centring on the auto industry, such as gas stations, auto loans and insurance, auto distribution and maintenance networks, have not developed – and all these services could generate much employment. In the US, according to their own statistics, the auto manufacturing industry accounts for 1.3 per cent of total employment, while auto-related service sectors account for 6.2 per cent. That is why we should open up the auto market in order to make local manufacturing competitive and lower import prices. This will accelerate the diffusion of private car ownership among ordinary Chinese families. This historical process will not only change the Chinese auto industry, but also the country's employment structure, with major implications for the future.

Gearing up for globalization

Fortunately, China has been implementing a policy of opening up to trade and investment flows for the past 23 years, that is, for longer than it took to negotiate China's accession to the WTO, and almost all Chinese have benefited from it. As a result of that policy, since 1977 China has doubled its income every ten years, while historically it took Britain 58 years, the US 47 years and Japan 35 years. This is why, during the negotiations, it was comparatively easy to convince our people that a gradual process of opening our market should not be regarded as unilateral concessions. The fact that the negotiations took longer than we expected has to some extent made it easier for us to prepare conceptually and in practical terms for WTO accession.

On the other hand, strong general public support to accession has been due to the fact that China, during the negotiations, has been very firm in protecting its fundamental interests. We need to make sure that the policy of opening up will not lead to mass unemployment; that it will not lead to the destruction of some key industries in China; and that it will not change China's national values, national culture and national identity. The opening of the market should be a positive element in China's economic development, not a negative factor.

Another strategic outcome of China's WTO accession is that it helped to get the Chinese people well prepared for economic globalization. It is generally believed in China that, confronted with the historical tide of economic globalization, China, like other countries, must participate actively in it. We must also participate *effectively* in order to benefit from this process and not to be harmed by it.

A country has to meet some basic conditions to be well placed for full participation:

1. First, it has to adopt a market-driven economic system: history has proved that countries that adopted command economies have never been an integral part of the world economy.
2. Second, it has to pursue an open-market policy. Countries that adopt protectionism and isolation will obviously not be able to take part in economic globalization.
3. Third, and probably most important, it has to promote economic development at home, with a relatively high rate of growth and sound macroeconomic management. Otherwise, one has no ability to compete and, what is worse, cannot mobilize the support of the general public behind active participation in economic globalization, since it will remain uncertain about what globalization will bring.

In conclusion, China's 15 years of negotiations have prepared us to participate in economic globalization in general, and for a new round of trade negotiations within the framework of the WTO in particular. We have discovered that a balanced approach between the opening-up policy and economic development works for China. The policy of opening up will serve economic development, which would not take place without a real opening-up policy. That is why we support a new round while facing the challenges of economic globalization; a new round that will bring stronger economic development for the world, and especially for the developing countries.

3
Implications of China's Accession for the Asia-Pacific Countries

Chae Wook and Han Hongyul

619 F14
P33

Accession to the World Trade Organization (WTO) will launch China into the global economy, accelerating its market-opening process. The expectation is that this will bring tremendous changes to the international economy as well as to China's. While developed countries like the United States, European Union (EU), Japan and Canada have been leading the world trade order so far, it is expected that developing countries, including China, will become much more influential in the multilateral trading system.

China will be able to strive to reach the state of an advanced economy with a new approach to the 'reform and open-door policy', which has been promoted since 1979. With the entry to the WTO, China will be forced to remove the barriers to trade and investment, improving market access for foreign capital and commodities. This will activate the market function; consequently, China's market will expand, and foreign enterprises will increasingly advance into it. In that process, some domestic industries may suffer from restructuring, while the overall Chinese economy will become more competitive.

Taking it into account that China has already been enjoying most-favoured-nation (MFN) status with 140 trading partners, it may not be able to achieve visible export increase for the time being. However, as the market expands in size and the market function works effectively, Chinese products will become more competitive internationally, in terms of price and non-price factors. Thus, Chinese upmarket, high-quality products will penetrate the world market. It is worth emphasizing, however, that such effects will come true only if China complies with the WTO rules and bound commitments.

China's entry into the WTO will have a critical impact on the global economy as well. Primarily, as China promotes 'reform and globalization', exports by other countries will rush to China. Then, competition among countries and firms to enter the huge Chinese market will create further trade, thereby contributing to the world economy. It is also conceivable that China will play an important role in strengthening the efficacy of world trade rules by reforming its domestic institutions in a way that is consistent with international norms.

However, China's entry to the WTO will sensibly affect its trading partners, particularly the developing countries. In the short run, developing countries will be able to improve their trade balance with China, as China accelerates its market-opening. In the long run, though, as Chinese products become more competitive in the world market, they are highly likely to make inroads in the markets of trading partners. Developing economies in the Asia-Pacific (AP) region may be the most affected, because their labour-intensive products will have to compete with Chinese commodities. Therefore, unless innovative reform is fostered by those countries, their exports will fall behind in competition, and economic growth will deteriorate.

World trade and the AP developing economies

In 1990–97, Asian trade grew faster than world trade as a whole, including both advanced and developing economies. World trade in manufactures grew most significantly during this period. Trade in machinery and transport equipment is unique, because it is the only sector in which trade by the advanced economies recorded the highest growth. The second-highest growth by both advanced economies and Asian economies was recorded in chemicals and chemical products. In all remaining products, the Asian economies were the most active traders. In short, world trade is becoming more and more concentrated in the advanced and Asian economies. This suggests that it is more and more plausible to explain international trade flows by theories based on technological aspects and economies of scale than by factor-endowment theory alone.

While it is true that developing economies have great stakes in the trade in manufactures, it is important to note that their shares fall very short of the average for the developed economies. The structure of trade by major trading groups is characterized by the following (Table 3.1):

- Machinery and transport equipment take the lion's share, followed by the 'other manufactured goods' of the Standard International

Table 3.1 Commodity structure of trade by region

SITC	Developed economies		Developing economies		EU		US		Japan		Developing Asia	
	Exp.	Imp.	Exp.	Imp.	Exp.	Imp.	Exp.	Imp.	Exp.	Imp.	Exp.	Imp.
0–9 Total	100	100	100	100	100	100	100	100	100	100	100	100
0 & 1 Food, live animals, beverages	7.5 (-0.8)	8.0 (-0.7)	8.6 (-1.8)	6.9 (-1.5)	8.5 (-0.7)	9.1 (-0.7)	7.4 (-2.3)	4.6 (-0.8)	0.5 (-0.1)	14.2 (-0.2)	5.4 (-2.1)	5.2 (-0.8)
2 & 4 Crude materials, oils and fats,	3.8 (-0.8)	4.1 (-0.9)	5.2 (-1.2)	4.9 (-0.8)	2.8 (-0.7)	4.2 (-0.9)	5.3 (-2.2)	2.7 (-0.2)	0.7 (0.0)	8.7 (-3.5)	4.2 (-1.2)	5.1 (-1.2)
3 Mineral, fuels and lubricants	3.8 (-0.4)	7.3 (-2.3)	15.0 (-11.6)	5.4 (-5.9)	2.9 (-0.7)	6.6 (-1.7)	1.9 (-1.4)	9.3 (-3.8)	0.5 (0.1)	11.1 (-7.0)	4.9 (-3.3)	4.8 (-5.9)
5 Chemicals	11.1 (0.7)	9.2 (0.6)	5.3 (0.9)	9.8 (0.0)	12.4 (0.7)	10.7 (0.7)	10.8 (0.4)	5.8 (1.1)	7.1 (1.6)	6.9 (0.0)	5.4 (1.0)	9.6 (-0.3)
7 Machinery and trans. equipment	44.4 (2.7)	39.4 (3.4)	30.9 (12.1)	42.3 (6.7)	41.3 (2.9)	37.0 (2.4)	50.3 (4.2)	46.8 (3.6)	69.1 (-1.6)	27.6 (8.9)	39.0 (10.5)	43.6 (7.3)
6 & 8 Other manufactures	26.0 (-1.9)	29.1 (-1)	33.2 (0.9)	27.8 (1.0)	29.2 (-2.9)	29.4 (-1.4)	20.5 (1.6)	28.2 (-0.1)	19.3 (-1.2)	29.2 (2.0)	38.8 (-5.7)	28.7 (0.2)

Note: Numbers in brackets indicate % change in 1995-98.
Source: International Trade Statistics (1999).

Trade Classification (SITC 6 and 8). The developed economies' export share of machinery and transport equipment (44.4 per cent) greatly exceeds the world average (39.5 per cent), though their export share of other manufactured goods fall little short of the average

- This pattern is most conspicuous in US and Japanese trade; their export and import shares of machinery and transport are even greater than the average for all developed economies, while those of other manufactured goods are far below them
- In contrast, the developing Asian economies are net importers of transport equipment. Yet Asian developing economies have increased their share of machinery exports by 10.5 per cent in 1995–98, while their share of 'other manufactured products' decreased by 5.7 per cent
- Import shares of machinery and transport equipment increased significantly and uniquely. Developing economies need to enhance their export structures in consistence with structural changes in world trade. They are moving in right direction, but there still is a long way to go

This observation contradicts the traditional view that the liberalization of trade in manufactures is just in the interest of the developed countries. In fact, exports of manufactures account for almost three-quarters of all developing-country exports. Such a change in the structure of merchandise exports has potentially important implications for the AP developing economies following China's accession to the WTO. Not only do the average developing economies gain from the liberalization of the Chinese market, but also, as a group including China, would have a greater stake in the next round of multilateral trade negotiations for the liberalization of these products.

Of course, the export structures of the AP developing economies are not homogeneous. The differences between them will lead to differential impacts on their exports to the Chinese market (Table 3.2).

South

- South AP economies are relatively dependent on primary exports. The exports of primary products (SITC 0) accounted for 16.88 per cent in India and 19.83 per cent in Sri Lanka – significantly higher shares than those of other AP economies, except Thailand's (18.08 per cent)
- In Bangladesh, garments are a dominant export industry. In 1998, textiles and clothing accounted for more than 80 per cent of total exports, taking over from jute, which recorded about 6 per cent

40

Table 3.2 Export structure of AP developing economies
Selected countries, by commodity group, 1990–97

Exports	0		1		2		3		4		5		6		7		8		9	
	1997		1997		1997		1997		1997		1997		1997		1997		1997		1997	
India	16.8	2.9	0.46	-0.4	4.9	-4.9	1.7	-1.3	0.8	0.55	8.1	0.7	39.1	1.8	7.48	0.06	19.1	1.6	0.8	-0.4
Sri Lanka	19.8	-12.9	1.23	0.9	4.2	-3.5	0.7	-0.8	0	-0.4	0.87	-0.15	15.5	2.1	2.56	-0.3	53.2	1.9	17.2	-2.3
Indonesia	7.56	-1.3	0.46	-0.1	10.2	3.5	25.8	-17.9	3.2	1.52	3.46	1.14	21.8	-2.1	10.0	8.7	17.4	0.2	6.96	-0.3
Thailand	18.0	-10.1	0.36	-0.03	4.5	-1.2	2.2	1.3	0.1	0.09	3.71	2.29	15.5	-2.9	39.2	16.9	13.4	2.98	-8.1	1.8
Rep of Korea	1.95	-1.1	0.14	-0.05	1.3	-0.2	3.9	2.9	0.03	0.03	7.83	3.97	21.4	-0.7	50.0	10.7	8.84	4.59	-19.7	4.3
China	6.05	-4.5	0.57	0.02	2.3	-3.4	3.8	-4.6	0.35	0.09	5.6	-0.4	18.8	-1.4	23.9	14.9	38.6	0	18.1	-18.7
Singapore	1.73	-1.1	1.49	0.03	1.0	-2.1	8.7	-9.4	0.27	-0.5	6	-0.27	5.6	-1.4	65.9	15.8	7.7	1.5	-1.2	0.2

Note: Numbers in the right columns of each economy indicate % change in 1990–97.

- In India, the share of primary exports increased by 2.95 per cent during the period, while share increases of major manufactured goods (SITC 6, 7, 8) remained at about 1 per cent. Export shares of light-industry products (such as leather, rubber and machines) and miscellaneous manufactured articles (such as apparel and footwear) are 39.06 per cent and 19.07 per cent, respectively – while those for Sri Lanka are 15.50 per cent and 53.19 per cent
- One of the characteristics worth noting on the export structure of South AP economies is that it is highly concentrated, and shows no sign of improving

Southeast

- Southeast Asian economies have similar export structures. Although exports of manufacturing goods are most important, primary exports also have significant shares. However, the export structure of this subgroup's economies is in a process of a rapid change
- In Thailand, the share of primary exports decreased by more than 10 percentage points during the last decade, while that of machinery and transport equipment (SITC 7) increased by almost 17 points
- Indonesia's exports of these products increased by 8.7 points, though the contraction of primary exports was relatively small
- In the Philippines, merchandise exports and their contribution to gross domestic product (GDP) increased significantly. Also, the export structure continued to shift from primary to manufactured products, with the share of the latter reaching 86 per cent in 1997. Major exports include electronics, automotive products and apparel

Middle-income

- The export structure of middle-income Asian economies is quite different from other AP developing economies. For instance, the Republic of Korea's exports are concentrated in machinery and transport equipment (SITC 7), and the total share of manufacture exports is above 90 per cent. Between 1997 and 1990, the share of heavy industry gained 10.7 points while that of light industrial products shrank considerably

China's liberalization schedule

Basic policy directions

China considers the first decade of the twenty-first century as a strategic period in its march towards advanced-economy status. Since China promulgated its first explicit industrial policy in 1989, its economic policies have been oriented towards industrial restructuring. While striving to strengthen agriculture by developing the rural economy, it has promoted the development of so-called 'pillar' industries – machinery, electronics, petroleum, raw chemicals, automobiles and construction. Industrial restructuring has been also been related to foreign trade. The foreign trade policy has encouraged exports of agricultural products with comparative advantages, home electronic appliances, and some high value-added products. Encouragement was also given to imports of crucial parts, equipment and technologies. As a result, China's trade volume has grown to the point that it has become the ninth-largest trading nation in the world. Furthermore, as China has been successfully transforming its economy from a centrally planned autarky into a market-based system, it has become fairly open to trade and investment. Since the early 1990s, China has gradually cut its tariff rate from above 40 per cent to the current 15 per cent. As for non-tariff barriers (NTBs), after promulgation of the landmark Law of Foreign Trade of the People's Republic of China in 1994, China accelerated the elimination of licence requirements and of most import quotas, and introduced an automatic import licensing system.[1]

In its bid for membership of the WTO, China has made comprehensive commitments to liberalize trade and investment, so with accession, many of the remaining trade barriers are expected to be further lowered or removed, and foreign enterprises in China will have a better chance to gain 'national treatment'.[2]

China's Five-Year Plan (FYP) for National Economic and Social Development and the Long-Term Target for the Year 2010 defines the new directions of state intervention and provide a blueprint of national development into the twenty-first century. These can be summarized as follows:[3]

- GDP to double the year 2000 figure
- Contain population to 1.4 billion and enable people to lead an 'even more comfortable life'
- Establish 'a relatively complete socialist market economy', a sounder macro-economic control system with better agility and effectiveness, and a regulatory framework more in compliance with the rule of law
- Establish a modern enterprise system for state-owned enterprises (SOEs) and develop a number of internationally competitive large enterprises and business groups

- Optimize industrial structure by:
  - Enhancing commercialization and specialization in agriculture
  - Building up a group of national infrastructure projects and matching development of infrastructure and basic industries to national economic growth
  - Promoting pillar industries and making them the major driving force of economic growth
  - Increasing markedly the proportion of the tertiary sector in the national economy and its service function
- Promote a more coordinated development of regional economies and gradually narrow the gap in development between different regions

According to these outlines, economic reform and industrial restructuring must be China's main policy instruments to ensure a sustainable and rapid economic growth in the globalized economy. Specifically, institution-building for a market economy and development of the 'pillar industries' will be at the top of the policy agenda in coming years. Furthermore, it is expected that China will accelerate the plan upon its entry to the WTO in response to the comprehensive market-opening. A shift will take place from the centrally planned economy to the socialist market economy, where the market plays a fundamental role in resource allocation, and from an quantitative growth mode to an qualitative growth mode, driven by increasing efficiency and productivity.

Overview of the US–China agreement's provisions on industry and services

By joining the WTO, China is committing itself to establishing a 'tariff-only' import regime; all NTBs will be eliminated. Any other measure, such as inspection, testing, and domestic taxes must be applied in a manner that is consistent with WTO rules that require a transparent and non-discriminatory system, and all health measures must be based on sound science.

On 15 December 1999, China successfully concluded bilateral negotiations with the US,[4] which established benchmarks for the agreement with the WTO. What follows is a summary of the most relevant points of the agreement as relates to industry and services.

Industrial products

China has made a comprehensive commitment to reduce tariff and NTBs in the industrial sector (Table 3.3). The average tariff rates are to

Table 3.3   Industrial products: tariff reduction schedule
Unit: %

Items	Current rates	Rates to be reduced	Due years
Averages	17	9.4	2005
Automobiles	80–100	25	2006
Auto parts	23.4	10	2005
IT products	13	0	1 January 2005
Civil aircraft	14.7	8	1 January 2002
Construction equipments	13.6	6.4	1 January 2004
Medical equipments	9.9	4.7	1 January 2003
Scientific equipments	12.3	6.5	1 January 2003
Pharmaceuticals	9.6	4.2	1 January 2003
Chemicals	14.74	6.9	1 January 2005
Fertilizers	6	4	Upon accession
Cosmetics	45	10 or 15	2004 or 2005
Textiles and apparel	25.4	11.7	1 January 2005
Steel products	10.3	6.1	1 January 2003
Furniture	22	0	1 January 2005
Lumber	15–25	12–18	1 January 2005
Paper and paper products	14.2	5.5	1 January 2005

Source: USTR (1999a).

be reduced to 9.4 per cent, with some major items to be lowered to 7.1 per cent and quotas in general to be eliminated by 2002, or at the latest by 2005.

The most remarkable changes are in the areas of autos and information technology (IT) products. Other items which are mostly of concern to developed countries – such as aircraft, equipment and pharmaceuticals – will also undergo substantial tariff reduction. Changes in tariffs on products such as chemicals, furniture, paper, steel and textiles are of concern to developing countries in general.

Autos and IT

- China will lower the tariff rates of *automobiles* from 80–100 per cent to 25 per cent by 2006 after accession, cutting those of related *major components* from 23.4 per cent to 10 per cent, and eliminating the import quota system by 2005
- *Quotas on autos* will be phased out by 2005, growing 15 per cent annually until eliminated (Table 3.4)
- China agreed to sign the IT Agreement (ITA) on accession, thereby committing itself to eliminate tariffs on all *products covered by the ITA* by 1 January 2005

Table 3.4   Autos: tariff reduction schedule
Unit: %

Rate	2000	2001	2002	2003	2004	2005	1/2006	7/2006
100	77.5	61.7	50.7	43.0	37.6	30.0	28.0	25.0
80	63.5	51.9	43.8	38.2	34.2	30.0	28.0	25.0

Source: USTR (1999a).

Of concern to developed nations

- For *civil aircraft*, tariffs on all items in Annex 1 of the Agreement on Trade in Civil Aircraft (ATCA) will be bound and reduced form the current average rate of 14.7 per cent to a final average rate of 8 per cent starting upon China's accession and with most restrictions completed by 1 January 2002
- *Quotas and licences* will be eliminated upon accession for all items in the ATCA
- Tariffs on *construction, medical and scientific equipment* are to be more than halved, from 13.6 per cent to 6.4 per cent, by 1 January 2004, from 9.9 per cent to 4.7 per cent by 1 January 2003, and from 12.3 per cent to 6.5 per cent by 1 January 2003
- China will reduce its average tariff on *pharmaceuticals* by 60 per cent from its current average tariff of 9.6 per cent to 4.2 per cent by 1 January 2003

Of concern to developing nations

- China will reduce tariffs on *chemicals* by more than 50 per cent by 1 January 2005, with the average rate of 14.74 per cent falling to 6.9 per cent. Specifically, China will reduce its tariffs on *fertilizers and cosmetics*, from 6 per cent to 4 per cent upon accession and from around 45 per cent to 10 per cent or 15 per cent by 2004 or 2005, respectively. Tariff reductions on chemicals involve full implementation of more than two-thirds of the products in the Tariff Harmonization Agreement of the Uruguay Round (UR)
- Average tariff on *textiles and apparel* (probably the products of greatest concern to developing countries) will be reduced from 25.4 per cent to 11.7 per cent, starting on accession and finalizing by 1 January 2005
- Most quotas on *priority US exports* will be eliminated upon accession (except those on thirty *yarn, synthetic filament tow, and fibre products*, which will be eliminated after one year)

- Tariffs on *steel and steel products* (another important item to some developing countries) will be reduced from 10.3 per cent to 6.1 per cent by 1 January 2003
- A striking tariff reduction is to be made on *furniture* items: the current average tariff rate of 22 per cent will be reduced to zero on all furniture items covered by the UR sectoral initiative. Reduction will commence upon accession and will be fully implemented by 1 January 2005
- Tariffs on *lumber* will be lowered from 15–25 per cent to 12–18 per cent, and those on *paper and paper products* will be reduced from 14.2 per cent to 5.5 per cent by 1 January 2005

Services

China has made commitments to phase out most restrictions in a broad range of service sectors, including telecommunications, distribution, banking and insurance, professional services such as accountancy and legal consulting, and audiovisual services (Table 3.5).

Telecommunications

- Geographical limitation on *beepers and value-added services* will be lifted within two years of accession, those on personal communication services (PCS) within six years
- *Foreign suppliers* are allowed to hold 30 per cent foreign equity share upon accession, 49 per cent after one year, 50 per cent after two years in the area of *value-added services*
- Foreign suppliers will be also able to provide *all analogue/digital cellular services and PCs*, and they are allowed to hold 25 per cent foreign equity share one year after accession, 35 per cent after three years, and 49 per cent after five years of accession
- While there is no specific commitment or relevant domestic rules on regarding *portal-site management and provision of content*, the Chinese government has been publicizing the plan to open those markets in the form of joint-ventures

Distribution

- Restrictions on all products in distribution services will be phased out within three years. Foreign service suppliers will be permitted to establish joint-ventures within one year of accession, and foreign majority equity share will be allowed, with all geographical and quantitative restrictions eliminated, within two years after accession[5]

Table 3.5   Major service sectors: liberalization schedule

Sectors	Foreign equity shares	Geographical limitations
Telecommunication		
Value-added service	30% upon accession, 49% after one year, 50% after two years (of accession)	No restrictions after two years (of accession)
Mobile voice and data services	25% after one year, 35% after two year, 49% after five years	No restrictions after five years (of accession)
Domestic and international services	25% after three years, 35% after five years, 49% after six years	No restrictions after five years (of accession)
Distribution		
Wholesale and commission agents services	Joint-ventures within one year, foreign majority equity share within two years, wholly-owned subsidiaries within three years	No restrictions within two years
Retails	No restrictions within three years	No restrictions within three years
Franchizing	No restrictions within three years	No restriction within three years
Banking	Licensed with thresholds and choose legal form after five years	
Insurance		
Non-life insurance	Branch 51% upon accession, wholly-owned subsidiary within two years	No restrictions within three years
Life insurance	50% upon accession	No restrictions within three years

Source: USTR (1999a).

- Even in retailing services, within three years from the date of accession, there will be no restrictions on equity, geographic areas, or on the number of service suppliers

Banking
- *Local currency business* with foreign clients will be permitted upon accession; with Chinese enterprises two years after; and with Chinese individuals five years after accession
- Regarding *geographic restrictions*, local currency banking will be permitted in four cities upon accession, four additional cities will be

permitted each year thereafter, and nationwide access five years after accession. However, foreign currency business will be allowed without geographic restrictions on accession

- China will phase out all geographic restrictions on the *insurance* market within three years of accession. In particular, joint-ventures with partner of choice at 50 per cent equity share will be permitted upon accession for life insurance. While foreign service suppliers of non-life insurance will be permitted to establish branches and joint-ventures at 51 per cent equity share upon accession, wholly-owned subsidiaries will be permitted within a year from date of accession

Other services

- China has agreed on market access and national treatment for *accounting, auditing and bookkeeping* services. Foreign accounting firms will be permitted to affiliate with Chinese firms and enter into contractual agreements with their affiliated firms in other WTO member countries. These firms must be represented by Certified Public Accountants (CPA) licensed by Chinese authorities; however, existing accounting firms are exempted from this requirement. CPA licences will be issued on a national treatment basis where applicants will be informed of results in writing no later than 30 days after submission of their application
- For *legal services*, foreign firms will be able to provide services in the form of a profit-making representative office, giving advice on international conventions and practices, and the law of other WTO members in which the lawyer is licensed to practice. While they are not allowed to employ Chinese nationals as lawyers for the practice of Chinese law, they can enter into long-term 'entrustment' contracts providing for close working relationships with firms practising Chinese law.[6] All geographic and quantitative restrictions will be phased out within one year of China's accession, which means that foreign firms can open more than one office anywhere in China
- An agreement was also made to open the Chinese *audiovisual* market. Foreign service suppliers will be permitted to establish joint-ventures with equity share up to 49 per cent to distribute audiovisuals. Furthermore, 40 movies will be imported upon accession, while 50 movies will be imported within three years

Trade-related investment measures (TRIMs)

China's commitments to eliminate NTBs and certain conditions on exports and investment all enter into effect immediately upon China's accession to the WTO. According to these, China will eliminate the requirements of foreign-exchange balance, local contents and export performance, implementing the WTO agreement on TRIMs. China has also agreed that the government will not condition its approval of an investment on whether a company provides offsets, transfers technology, uses locally produced goods, or conducts research and development (R&D) in China. In addition, China has confirmed the application of WTO rules to SOEs and extended those disciplines to state-invested enterprises where the government has an equity interest. Under these commitments, China's state-owned and state-invested enterprises are required to buy and sell based on commercial considerations, such as quality and price.

Assessing the liberalization schedule

The benchmark deal on US–China trade promises to open up one of the world's largest economies to unprecedented foreign competition. China has committed itself to a substantial reduction of tariffs and to remove most quotas on both agricultural and industrial products. Many sectors previously considered off-limits, including banking and telecommunications, will be forced to prepare for competition from bigger and stronger foreign companies in two to five years.

While China maintained high tariff rates of 40 per cent or higher in early 1990s, these were substantially reduced to an average of 16.8 per cent by 1999. The tariff rates will be further reduced to 10 per cent by 2005 under the agreement. Some researchers have estimated that such tariff cuts will bring about an increase in China's imports of about US$18–20 billion in 2005.[7] So, in that year China's trade volume is expected to exceed US$600 billion, almost twice the level of 1998. Furthermore, as China establishes a 'tariff-only' import regime by eliminating quotas on most products, the price mechanism will work effectively through the market, benefiting consumers with a wider choice of products at cheaper prices. A more striking and surprising outcome from the deal is China's comprehensive commitment to phase out restrictions in a broad range of service sectors over a relatively short period. It is striking because foreign service business in China is strictly limited. For example, China currently not only limits foreign banks to foreign currency business in selected cities and to foreign customers only, but also permits foreign securities firms to trade only a limited number of stocks. Similarly, China allows selected insurance companies to operate in China on a limited basis in two cities. Furthermore, foreign service suppliers are barred from providing telecom services in China, and companies are generally barred from distributing imported products or providing related distribution services such as repair and maintenance services. Such restrictions on service sectors will start to be removed upon accession to the WTO, and will be phased out over the ensuing five years.

The US as main beneficiary

While these liberalization measures will certainly benefit almost all of China's trading partners, it is highly likely that the developed countries, and particularly the US, will gain the most. This is so, because the commitments were made to favour the products or services of US priority interest.

For example, the average tariff rates on agricultural products of US priority interest are to be reduced from 31 per cent to 14 per cent, while the overall average rates decline from 22 per cent to 17.5 per cent. Furthermore, China will be required to eliminate export subsidies and provide increased import quotas on wheat, corn, rice and cotton for the US.

Similarly, while overall average tariff rates are to be reduced from 17 per cent to 9.4 per cent, those on the major products in which the US has the priority interest will fall to 7.1 per cent. Autos, aircraft, medical or scientific equipment, and pharmaceuticals are typical examples.

China's liberalization schedule will certainly favour the US even in relation to service sectors, because China has committed itself to open up mostly the service sectors in which the US have comparative advantage. As a result, it is expected that the US banks, insurers, telecommunications firms and film exporters will rush to China after its accession to the WTO in order to capture its huge market. However, other developed countries will also gain from China's market opening because they have, in general, industrial structures similar to that of the US.

What the developing countries can expect

Developing countries will obtain benefits directly and indirectly from China's liberalization. As the US and other developed countries increase their exports of value-added products to China, its demand for raw materials will surge, allowing developing countries to expand their exports of raw materials or related intermediate goods. The prices of those materials or intermediate goods may rise, as the issues of environmental protection or preservation of natural resources become priority concerns (see Chapter 5). This will give developing countries more favourable terms of trade in international markets. Such effects are expected mainly for products such as textiles, steel, lumber, paper and furniture – but may also extend to the exports of some agricultural products, particularly specialty crops, to China.

However, the liberalization of China's service sectors may not directly affect developing economies, at least in the short run. The only possibility is that it may induce more foreign direct investment (FDI) from developed countries that are willing to take advantage of cheaper rents or labour costs as well as geographical location.

The industrial structure of South Asian economies support this view. The shares of primary products in total value added are 32 per cent, 25 per cent, 22 per cent and 18 per cent, respectively, in Bangladesh, India, Pakistan and Sri Lanka. On the other hand, the financial and transport and communication sectors take less than 10 per cent in total. Since exports by South Asian countries are centred mostly on some primary and labour-intensive manufactures, the benefits from China's liberalization would be greatest in the related areas. For example, more than a half of Pakistan's exports are cotton-based products. The situation is more or less similar in other South Asian countries; exports of some manufactures, particularly light industrial products, take a dominant share.

While the situation is quite different in some countries of other Asian regions such as Singapore, Chinese Taipei and the Republic of Korea, it is expected that the liberalization of China's service sectors will have minimal impact on most developing economies when the competitiveness of their service industries is considered. There is another challenge for the AP developing economies in general. China's accession to the WTO ensures that the Multi-Fibre Agreement (MFA) quota, hitherto imposed annually, will be abolished by 2005. Though it is not clear who will be the winner in the freer trading environment for textiles and clothing, major exporters of these products in this region will be exposed to a fiercer competition with China. While the MFA quota is already in the process of elimination, it is still too early to assess the effects because no meaningful liberalization has yet taken place. Presumably, the elimination of the MFA quota would divide the developing countries into higher-cost and lower-cost suppliers. For instance, the Republic of Korea, Chinese Taipei and Hong Kong SAR, China will be most negatively affected because they currently have a fairly substantial quota and relatively high wage rates. Of course, it is also possible that the new and small suppliers could be squeezed out with the abolition of the protection provided by the MFA quota. This argument is based on the productivity difference between large quota holders and small suppliers.[8]

These considerations demand more detailed analysis of the impact China's WTO accession will have on the AP developing economies. First, we look at which areas or commodities are of major export interest for the AP developing economies – analyzing their shares in the world's major export markets and respective comparative advantages. Second, we analyze in detail how the tariff liberalization affects the exports of AP developing economies to the Chinese market. The analysis is based on the US–China bilateral agreement. Third, we consider the issue of trade in textiles and clothing, because the eliminations of MFA quotas will make one of the most immediate and foreseeable impacts on the exports of AP developing economies.

Impact on AP developing economies

Areas of export interest

China's import market is dominated by few suppliers – chiefly Japan, the US, Chinese Taipei and the Republic of Korea. Their combined share of China's imports is above 60 per cent. In the US, EU and Japan, the top five suppliers' combined share is around 50 per cent (Table 3.6). The concentration in China's structure is mainly attributable to significantly high shares of Japan, the Republic of Korea and Chinese Taipei, which are geographically closest to China, which suggests that an explanation based on the gravity model of trade flows may be relevant.

The performance of AP economies in the Chinese market differs greatly. While India takes 0.94 per cent of the US market, it only has

Table 3.6   Top five suppliers in major markets (1998)
Unit: %

Markets	Top 5 suppliers				
US	Canada (18.41)	Japan (13.44)	Mexico (10.15)	China (8.17)	Germany (5.39)
EU	US (17.56)	Japan (10.31)	China (6.99)	Germany (5.42)	Canada (5.30)
Japan	US (23.99)	China (13.35)	Australia (4.68)	Rep of Korea (4.30)	Indonesia (3.90)
China	Japan (20.16)	US (12.03)	Chinese Taipei (11.85)	Rep of Korea (10.7)	Germany (5.0)

Source: UNCTAD Trains (2000).

Table 3.7 Market shares of AP economies in major markets
Unit: %

	Bangladesh	India	Pakistan	Indonesia	Malaysia	Philippines	Thailand	Chinese Taipei	Rep of Korea
US	0.21	0.94	0.20	1.09	2.12	1.32	1.52	3.70	2.68
EU	1.39	1.39	0.34	1.27	1.62	0.63	1.33	2.65	2.17
Japan	0.04	0.79	0.11	3.90	3.04	1.56	2.83	3.53	4.30
China	0.02	0.64	0.28	1.75	1.90	0.37	1.72	11.85	10.7

Source: UNCTAD Trains (2000).

an 0.64 per cent share in the Chinese market. Except for Pakistan and Indonesia, other South and Southeast AP economies have significantly higher shares in major export markets than in the Chinese market (Table 3.7).

In contrast, the Republic of Korea and Chinese Taipei show dramatically different bilateral trade flows with China from those of other AP developing economies. The Republic of Korea's import share in the Chinese market is 10.7 per cent, while it is less than 3 per cent in the US market; Chinese Taipei's share reaches almost 12 per cent, while its share in the US is only 3.7 per cent. This pattern of bilateral trade flows between AP developing economies and China sheds some light on the possible effects of China's liberalization policy.

Small suppliers in South Asian economies may expect greater opportunities in the Chinese market. If Bangladesh can take 0.21 per cent of market share in the US, it would be simply unreasonable to assume that its share will remain at the current level after liberalization of the Chinese market. It is a price-elasticity issue; exports by these economies competing with domestic suppliers will have better price competitiveness after China's tariff cuts.

We noted earlier that the world economy is fast concentrating on high value-added and capital-intensive products. China's import structure seems to follow the global trends (Figure 3.1). Therefore, for AP

Figure 3.1 China's import structure

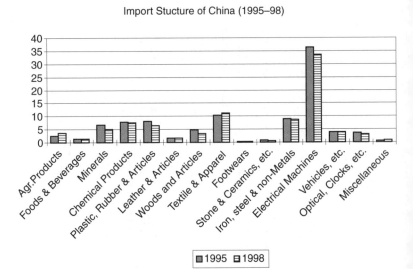

Import Stucture of China (1995–98)

☐1995 ☐1998

developing economies to catch up with the development process of advanced economies, they may have to align their industrial and export structures to be consistent, in the long run, with the changes in world trade structure. In order to examine to what extent China's accession to WTO would create export opportunities for AP developing economies, we have to consider the impact of its liberalization plan on the product-specific export performance of these economies in China.

The stakes of different groups of AP developing economies in the Chinese market differ from those they have in the US market (Table 3.8). South Asian economies have limited market shares in manufactures (SITC 6–8) in China, while they have meaningful shares in the US. For example, while India's market shares of manufactures in the US are 3.24 per cent and 1.59 per cent for SITC 6 and 8, respectively, its shares in China are insignificant. Even in the category of SITC 7 (machinery and transport equipment), India's relatively limited share in the US is four times bigger than that in China. Conversely, India's share of primary products in China is about six times bigger than that in the US. This suggests that these countries would gain much from the liberalization of primary products by China. Manufactures may be another area of interest for India, considering its recent significant increase of shares in both markets.

The export structures of Southeast Asian economies show an interesting pattern. Indonesia, Thailand and Malaysia have greater shares in the Chinese market in many products. For instance, Malaysia has higher US market shares in machinery and other manufactured goods, while its market share for all other products is lower than in China.

The relative positions of AP developing economies in the Chinese market also emerge from examining their export competitiveness, as measured by revealed comparative advantage (RCA). (Table 3.9 shows the situation in 1998.) As an RCA of one implies better export performance of a product relative to a country's overall exports, products with RCA higher than one can be said to 'reveal' comparative advantage in the export market in question. Overall, Southeast and South Asia economies have a similar group of products in which comparative advantages are revealed.

Common areas in which they have RCAs higher than unity include: food and animals (SITC 0), raw materials (SITC 2), animal and vegetable oils (SITC 4). The main difference between the two country groups is that Indonesia and the Philippines reveal comparative advantage in mineral fuels while the South Asian countries show strong competitiveness in manufactured goods. However, the contrast needs more scrutiny, because the latter product group includes a wide variety of industrial products from textiles and apparel to iron and steel. We

Table 3.8 AP economies' market shares in China and US
By commodity

China	0	1	2	3	4	5	6	7	8	9
Bangladesh	0.17		0.13	0.04			0.03	0.00	0.03	
Pakistan	0.22	0.05	0.15			0.00	1.16	0.18	0.00	
Indonesia	2.35	0.29	4.20	6.83	8.41	1.16	3.14	1.55	0.18	
Malaysia	0.69	0.82	2.71	1.85	32.81	1.27	1.77	1.66	0.47	0.01
Thailand	5.89	0.03	2.71	0.87	0.07	2.51	1.08	0.38	0.53	0.01
Philippines	1.89	1.82	0.19	0.67	2.19	0.13	0.30		0.11	
Singapore	0.28	0.63	0.19	13.82	0.63	2.93	0.52	3.96	2.23	8.22
Rep of Korea	1.96	0.67	4.88	16.01	0.29	18.36	18.28	5.77	7.60	0.49
Chinese Taipei	0.68		4.64	0.60	0.28	16.22	19.96	9.95	10.57	0.48

US	0	1	2	3	4	5	6	7	8	9
Bangladesh	0.26	0.01	0.01			0.00	0.08	0.00	1.02	
India	1.77	0.20	1.49	0.00	2.63	0.84	3.24	0.12	1.59	0.00
Pakistan	0.09	0.00	0.05			0.00	0.69	0.00	0.53	
Indonesia	2.85	0.40	3.36	0.79	4.71	0.23	1.19	0.49	2.22	0.00
Malaysia	0.32	0.03	0.97	0.38	12.88	0.46	0.48	3.46	1.55	0.27
Thailand	5.39	0.55	1.41	0.76	0.06	0.16	1.02	1.48	4.08	0.00
Philippines	1.38	0.10	0.16	0.00	19.07	0.06	0.25	1.80	1.77	0.01
Singapore	0.36	0.02	0.11	0.31	0.44	0.67	0.12	3.66	0.66	
China	2.24	0.48	2.59	0.71	0.53	2.82	6.37	5.19	23.85	0.13
Rep of Korea	0.39	0.24	0.88	0.35	0.07	1.35	3.15	3.53	2.37	0.14
Taiwan Prov	0.98	0.23	0.60	0.76	0.24	0.87	3.80	4.90	4.08	0.01

Table 3.9 Revealed comparative advantages of AP economies in China (1998)

SITC	0	1	2	3	4	5	6	7	8	9
Bangladesh	8.50	0.0	6.5	0.0	0.0	0.0	1.50	0.0	1.50	0.0
India	10.1	0.02	4.67	0.08	3.41	0.38	1.11	0.03	0.30	0.03
Pakistan	0.79	0.0	0.54	0.14	0.0	0.0	4.14	0.0	0.0	0.0
Indonesia	1.34	0.03	2.40	3.90	4.81	0.66	1.79	0.1	0.10	0.0
Malaysia	0.36	0.15	1.43	0.97	17.27	0.67	0.93	0.82	0.25	0.01
Philippines	5.11	0.08	0.51	1.81	5.92	0.35	0.81	1.03	0.30	0.0
Thailand	3.42	0.48	1.58	0.51	0.04	1.46	0.63	0.97	0.31	0.01
Rep of Korea	0.18	0.06	0.46	1.50	0.03	1.72	1.71	0.54	0.71	0.05
Chinese Taipei	0.06	0.06	0.39	0.05	0.02	1.37	1.68	0.84	0.89	0.04

come back to this point further below. For the Republic of Korea and Chinese Taipei, products with RCA higher than one are limited to SITC 5 and 6, while the RCAs of SITC 7 and 8 are far below one. Compared to their export shares of SITC 7 and 8 in the US, they do not seem to fully exploit their export potential in the Chinese market.

The RCAs actually obscure real export prospects because SITC one-digit data contains various products which individual economies may not export at all. Also, AP economies may have prospects in some products that exceed those suggested by their RCA in China – if the export performance of those products is relatively good in other major markets.

In order to evaluate the effects of China's accession on AP developing economies, it is useful to list products for which these economies have either RCAs higher than one or a relatively high level of exports. For example, while RCAs of Korean exports for SITC 7 and 8 are considerably low in China, it is clear that those are Korea's major exports overall. In this context, we identify products of SITC at double-digit level for which AP economies might have good prospects in the Chinese market (Table 3.10).

Several patterns appear when the focus is adjusted in this manner:

- First, *South Asian economies* appear to have comparative advantages in primary products and light industrial products like leather products and textile (SITC 61, 65). Also, Bangladesh recorded some exports of apparel (SITC 84), while India exported a limited amount of industrial machines
- Second, the major exports of *Southeast Asian economies* include rubber, cork and wood, pulp, and various kinds of machineries. Particularly, Malaysia and Thailand recorded a significant amount of industrial equipment and data-processing machines. As regards Indonesia and the Philippines, petroleum and derivates, natural gas and vegetable oil are important areas of export to the Chinese markets
- Third, the exports of the *Republic of Korea and Chinese Taipei* to China are mostly industrial products ranging from SITC 61 to SITC 85. Also, petroleum products and processed natural gas are important export products for the Republic of Korea

Impact of tariff liberalization on the exports of AP developing economies

There are many technical difficulties involved in evaluating China's tariff liberalization in detail. For instance, since the US–China agree-

Table 3.10 Major areas of AP developing economies' export interest in the Chinese market

	1	2	3	4	5	6	7	8
0			Bangladesh India	Thailand	Phils. Thailand	Thailand		India
1								
2			Indonesia Malaysia Thailand	Indonesia Malaysia Thailand	Indonesia Thailand	Bangladesh India Indonesia Malaysia Thailand	India	India Thailand
3			Indonesia Phils. Sing. Rep of Korea Taiwan Prov	Indonesia Phils. Sing. Rep of Korea Taiwan Prov				
4		India Indonesia Malaysia Phils.						
5	Rep of Korea Taiwan Prov		Rep of Korea Taiwan Prov	Indonesia Rep of Korea Taiwan Prov	Bangladesh India Pakistan Indonesia Rep of Korea Taiwan Prov	India	Rep of Korea Taiwan Prov	
6	Bangladesh India Rep of Korea Pakistan Taiwan Prov		India Indonesia				Rep of Korea Taiwan Prov	

Table 3.10 Major areas of AP developing economies' export interest in the Chinese market (*continued*)

	1	2	3	4	5	6	7	8
7		India Malaysia Indonesia Thailand Phils. Rep of Korea Taiwan Prov	Malaysia Thailand Phils. Rep of Korea Sing. Taiwan Prov	Malaysia Thailand Phils. Rep of Korea Sing. Taiwan Prov	Malaysia Thailand Phils. Rep of Korea Taiwan Prov		Malaysia Indonesia Thailand Phils. Rep of Korea Sing. Taiwan Prov	
8	Indonesia Malaysia Thailand Rep of Korea Taiwan Prov			Bangladesh	Indonesia Thailand Rep of Korea Taiwan Prov			

Note: Each row represents SITC one-digit classification and each column represents SITC two-digit classification.

ment on tariff reduction is based on Harmonized System (HS) eight-digit level data, it is almost impossible to assess the tariff reduction schedule of each individual product. Also, as we are evaluating the areas of export prospects at SITC two-digit level, we have to measure representative tariff rates for each category by controlling tariff rates for affected HS items. Therefore, we have focused on products of export interest for AP developing economies at SITC two-digit level. We compiled trade-weighted MFN average tariffs and included products of HS six-digit level ranked among the top ten in import value. The products enjoying most significant tariff reduction (Table 3.11) include:

- Machinery and electrical machinery (SITC 72, 74, 75, 77, 78)
- Agricultural products (SITC 03)
- Textile fibres (SITC 26)
- Other products of light industry such as wood manufactures, paperboard, textile yarn and fabric, iron and steel (SITC 63,64, 65, 67)
- Miscellaneous manufactured articles like building fixtures, apparel and footwear (SITC 81, 84, 85)

Some items in which AP developing economies have some export interest (such as SITC 04, 05, 06,08 and 23) are not included in the China–US agreement. However, as the list of products of interest to AP developing economies includes most of the items listed above, China's liberalization schedule seems to be in conformity with the export interests of AP developing economies.

The expected expansion of imports is measured by applying implicit long-term price elasticity to the base year (1998) import values of individual products.[9] Significant increases in imports are expected for:

- Special industrial machines (SITC 72)
- Office and data-processing machines (SITC 75)
- Electrical equipment (SITC 77)

Except for Thailand and Indonesia, all economies have higher market shares of SITC 7 in the US market than in China. Although RCAs for these products are currently lower than one, significant tariff reduction on these products would provide good opportunities to East and Southeast Asian economies.

On the other hand, only limited expansion is expected for other export products from South Asian and Southeast Asian economies.

Table 3.11 Trade-weighted tariff reduction schedule and expected import expansion
Selected product groups (US$ 000, %)

SITC	Import value	Import expansion	Current rate	Bound rate	SITC	Import value	Import expansion	Current rate	Bound rate
0 0	54 417	0			53	1 122 383	n.a.	16.51	6.50
0 3	667 363	1 001.04	22.79	10.17	57	8 182 055	29 864.5	10.44	7.47
0 4	735 398	n.a.			61	1 991 442	9.5	13.09	4.93
0 5	353 673	n.a.			63	1 001 968	2 655.2	14.09	5.61
0 6	172 263	n.a.			64	3 423 184	22 079.5	18.59	8.97
0 8	1 405 060	n.a.			65	11 081 885	40.94	11.74	9.96
23	790 154	n.a.			66	1 409 532	19 592.4	10.05	5.81
24	975 363	2 389.6	3.40	1.22	67	6 488 848	6 164.4	12.11	2.50
25	1 094 518	1 587.1	1.00	0.10	72	8 294 663	116 954.7	10.64	8.25
26	2 401 785	81.7	14.48	7.14	73	2 596 283	36 607.5	14.98	6.98
27	270 754	1 827.6	3.73	3.70	74	6 284 194	88 607.1	10.31	0.45
28	3 293 609	6 587.2	2.00	1.37	75	6 036 217	150 301.8	9.97	3.70
33	5 882 205	16 470.2	4.53	3.19	77	16 683 891	83 419.4	26.14	11.49
34	824 040	1 112.4	6	3	78	1 986 130	9 930.65	20.20	13.68
42	1 384 565	18 553.17	25	15	81	108 417	64.9	32.82	15.77
51	3 491 868	19 379.8	10.33	5.57	84	1 071 925	1 822.2		

For example, the expected expansion for fish (SITC 03), cork and wood (SITC 24) and pulp (SITC 25) is estimated to be in the range of US$1–2 million. Therefore, we may conclude that China's liberalization schedule is biased towards imports of capital-intensive products and provides benefits to the relatively advanced economies in the AP region.

The situation becomes clearer when we look at the impact on exports by individual AP developing economies (Table 3.12). The extent of expected import expansion is limited for *South Asian economies*, mainly due to limited transactions between South Asia and East Asia in general. India is expected to have considerable opportunities only for the export of fixed vegetable oils (SITC 42) and non-metal mineral manufactures (SITC 66). However, it should be noted that the assessment of import expansion effects for individual economies could underestimate export opportunities because it is based on the current levels of market shares.

Currently insignificant exports to the Chinese market are one reason for the low expectations of import expansion for these economies. Considering the South Asian economies' significantly higher shares for their major exports in the US market, their potential may be greater than suggested by the current presence in the Chinese market of their light-industry manufactures. For instance, while Bangladesh had lost its share of the Chinese market for manufactured goods of SITC 6, India and Pakistan increased their shares noticeably during 1995–98.

Greater export opportunities are expected for *Southeast and East Asian economies*. First, Malaysia and the Philippines share the same prospects with India for exports of fixed vegetable oils. The expected increases amount to US$96 million for Malaysia and US$65 million for the Philippines. Second, all Southeast Asian economies are expected to gain from increased exports of electrical equipment (SITC 77). Also, Malaysia and Thailand will be able to increase considerably their exports of industrial equipment (SITC 74).

The Republic of Korea and Chinese Taipei seem to be the greatest beneficiaries of China's tariff liberalization. Brackets in which both economies can expect considerable export opportunities include: plastics (SITC 57), paper (SITC 64), textile yarn and fabrics (SITC 65), metalworking machinery (SITC 73), and industrial equipment (SITC 74). As far as the Republic of Korea is concerned, organic chemicals (SITC 51), special industrial equipment (SITC 72) and electrical equipment (SITC 77) are important.

Table 3.12 Export opportunities for individual AP developing economies in the Chinese market
By product (US$ 000)

SITC	South Asia			Southeast Asia				East Asia	
	Bangladesh	India	Pakistan	Malaysia	Thailand	Philippines	Indonesia	Rep of Korea	Taiwan Prov
03	11.0	26.5							
04									
05									
06									
08									
23				596.6	36.4		288.9		
24					1.7		37.65		
25					27.5		9.8		
26	2.0	9.5		10.6					
27		554.0							
28		762.0			30.8				
33						156.8	3 903.1	8 624.7	359.9
34						112.4	104.4	483.3	
42		654.2		96 853.0		6 305.9	24 404.4		
51								27 246.3	4 388.6
53									
57								50 517.7	40 731.1
61	2.3	10.5						255.5	191.5
63			3.5				5 128.1		
64							12 964.9	25 691.9	13 282.0
65	9.7	669.8	71.4				38.4	85.7	11.5
66									0
67		4 582.3						7 137.6	5 773.6

Table 3.12 Export opportunities for individual AP developing economies in the Chinese market (continued)
By product (US$ 000)

| | South Asia | | | Southeast Asia | | | | East Asia | |
SITC	Bangladesh	India	Pakistan	Malaysia	Thailand	Philippines	Indonesia	Rep of Korea	Taiwan Prov
72				1 126.9	243.9	102.3	214.7	14 323.4	40 501.3
73				899.4	397.0	136.7		15 983.1	58 011.1
74				4 761.6	6 356.1	186.9		36 039.4	2 018.3
75				735.5	3 174.9	369.6		766.04	
77				17 324.6	4 213.	3 644.8	1 585.	59 668.5	
78								1 719.1	4 210.3
81				14.9	12.4			13.4	22.5
84	60.4								

Competing with China: focus on textiles and apparel

The UR produced an agreement to eliminate the quantitative restrictions on trade in textiles and clothing imposed by the MFA. The phase-out of the MFA by 2004 is generally expected to expand exports from AP developing countries. However, China's accession to the WTO poses a major challenge to AP developing economies, as China and other textile exporting economies will have to face real competition with the abolition of bilateral MFA agreements.

In other words, the quota system of the MFA, whatever its intrinsic restrictive effects, has at least protected the allocated shares of textiles and apparel exports of individual exporting countries. The abolition of the quotas poses a new uncertainty: it could expose small but protected textiles and apparel suppliers to additional competition from other restrained exporters like China. Therefore, it is difficult to predict exactly what will happen as the MFA is phased out.

It is interesting to see what has happened among major US textiles and apparel suppliers in 1997–99 (Table 3.13). Most top suppliers lost their shares (except Mexico and Honduras, whose exports are preferentially treated in the US market). Considering their total market shares, the performance of AP developing economies is still impressive. For example, while Bangladesh's market share for all products is far less than 1 per cent, its textile share was above 5 per cent in 1999.

Table 3.13   Major suppliers of textiles and clothing to the US
Million sq. metres

Suppliers	Exports			Shares		
	1997	1998	1999	1997	1998	1999
Mexico	1 555.103	1 984.572	2 253.946	13.70	15.40	16.35
China	947.376	910.229	905.285	8.35	7.06	6.57
Honduras	725.982	798.962	889.254	6.40	6.20	6.45
Hong Kong SAR	736.450	862.439	825.912	6.49	6.69	5.99
Bangladesh	671.763	743.516	761.217	5.92	5.77	5.52
Chinese Taipei	589.586	620.643	629.124	5.19	4.82	4.56
Rep of Korea	320.484	460.075	521.518	2.82	3.57	3.78
Indonesia	393.554	433.677	429.858	3.47	3.37	3.12
India	315.584	364.260	378.998	2.78	2.83	2.75
Thailand	283.767	334.885	367.966	2.50	2.60	2.67
Sri Lanka	322.046	332.451	329.720	2.84	2.58	2.39
Pakistan	193.656	214.783	225.526	1.71	1.67	1.64
Malaysia	134.984	162.381	182.008	1.19	1.26	1.32

Source: US Department of Commerce.

In order to assess the impact of MFA phase-out and China's accession to the WTO on exports of AP developing economies, we must consider particular issues involved in textile trading under the MFA, such as quota-utilization ratio, quality upgrading and production-sharing activities.[10]

The *quota-utilization ratio* can be used to assess the extent to which the MFA actually restricts trade. Typically, the ratio is less than 100 per cent. However, it would be misleading to conclude that the MFA is less restrictive because the quota is not binding. First of all, quota allocation is usually made on the basis of the historical record, disregarding changes on the demand side. This results in disparities in quota utilization among suppliers. For example, the ratios of the Republic of Korea and Chinese Taipei remain at around 60 per cent, while those of other AP economies tend to be higher.

Also, as the quota allocation system allows limited flexibility between categories of textiles and clothing, there can easily exist both binding and non-binding quotas at the same time, leading to a lower utilization ratio (Table 3.14). Therefore, lower ratios may themselves reflect restrictions imposed on the textile trade by the MFA.

The fact that China's utilization ratio continued to decrease over the three years may be a sign of advances in the Chinese textile industry and its competitiveness, which could take full effect after the total phase-out of the MFA. For instance, the Chinese apparel industry is moving towards the production of quality-oriented and high-value-

Table 3.14   MFA quota utilization ratio, Asian suppliers

Suppliers	Quota Utilization Ratio		
	1997	*1998*	*1999*
Rep of Korea	49.45	62.07	62.29
China	81.74	77.23	76.63
Hong Kong SAR	54.08	65.82	61.26
Chinese Taipei	57.31	59.34	59.02
Singapore	23.76	22.31	25.12
Indonesia	82.00	89.75	79.30
Thailand	67.23	75.17	73.43
Malaysia	46.63	51.50	45.95
Philippines	61.94	61.90	65.14
Bangladesh	82.96	91.14	85.03
India	90.44	91.96	88.60
Sri Lanka	59.34	65.25	59.36
Pakistan	62.06	61.03	61.94

Source: US Department of Commerce.

added products. The change is led by producers in Hong Kong SAR, China, whose return to Chinese rule in 1997 has boosted China's textiles and apparel industry.[11] The US Trade Promotion Act (TPA) applies preferential tariffs to Central American and Caribbean countries. As a result, apparel imports from these countries are subject to the same rates as those from Mexico. It is expected that US exports of yarns and fabrics will expand by promoting production-sharing activities among the US wholesalers, producers and assembly lines in Central American and Caribbean countries. Therefore, the competitiveness of apparel produced by the production-sharing activities will greatly increase. In particular, the Act is expected to help compete with apparel imported from Asia.

Since the launch of the North American Free Trade Association (NAFTA), apparel imports from other NAFTA economies increased 585 per cent, while those from the Caribbean Basin and Asia increased about 250 per cent. Apart from China's accession to the WTO, the TPA has an important implication for AP developing economies: FDI may respond dramatically to this Act. This does not necessarily mean that capital will move from Asia to Central America – rather, that more FDI will head for other areas of Asia like Cambodia, Laos and Myanmar, which have strong comparative advantages in labour cost and quality.

In order to assess the competitiveness of AP developing economies in the US market for textiles and apparel, we conducted the constant market analysis (CMS) for 1997–98 (Tables 3.15 and 3.16). According

Table 3.15   Factors of export growth: MFA category total (US)

	Total growth	Growth effects	Product mix	Competitiveness
Rep of Korea	177.377	107.552	−35.308	105.134
China	92.322	200.148	−70.061	−37.669
Chinese Taipei	80.033	122.559	−37.88	−4.586
Indonesia	−67.442	100.399	−29.133	−138.658
Thailand	120.457	102.693	−32.699	50.512
Malaysia	58.004	27.14	−7.81	38.687
Philippines	109.682	81.945	−26.022	53.8
Cambodia	67.380	11.111	−3.03	58.669
Myanmar	27.394	4.709	−1.392	23.907
Vietnam	6.263	1.784	−0.33	6.82
Macau	51.662	23.279	−6.74	35.134
Bangladesh	44.982	89.15	−24.024	−20.1
India	65.784	111.616	−28.108	−17.667
Sri Lanka	32.402	54.347	−15.874	−6.044
Pakistan	61.125	152.786	−34.896	−56.761

Table 3.16 Factors of export growth: total apparel (US)

	Total growth	Growth effects	Product mix	Competitiveness
Rep of Korea	404.429	204.412	−47.451	247.566
China	−59.434	523.736	−71.181	−511.74
Chinese Taipei	72.528	299.349	−112.251	−114.428
Indonesia	52.258	213.762	−99.686	−61.715
Thailand	228.442	192.144	−87.006	243.853
Malaysia	83.013	59.623	−28.405	51.823
Philippines	246.191	164.768	−76.582	158.083
Cambodia	145.089	7.541	−4.258	140.559
Myanmar	42.76	7.589	−3.382	38.311
Vietnam	8.841	3.686	−2.22	6.58
Macau	101.197	44.119	−21.58	78.68
Bangladesh	146.009	191.128	−105.058	60.03
India	163.693	246.435	−157.02	74.395
Sri Lanka	80.663	119.844	−53.034	13.91
Pakistan	418.637	281.461	−169.169	306.332

to the CMS model, the proportionate increase in exports of a commodity over time is composed of the following factors: market-growth effect, product-mix effect and residual effects which might reflect price competitiveness, quality changes and managerial skills.

There seems to be a common pattern. All suppliers responded quickly to changes in demand growth – though the negative signs on the product-mix effect imply that Asian economies did not catch up very well with changes in demand structure. Economies differ from each other regarding the residual 'competitiveness' effects. The positive signs for the Republic of Korea and Chinese Taipei seem to be attributable to price competitiveness resulting from the drastic depreciation of their currencies after the crisis.

One of the most interesting aspects of this exercise is that the less developed Southeast Asian economies showed impressive competitiveness – indeed, the competitiveness factor contributed to most of their export growth. On the contrary, South Asian economies are heavily dependent on the growth of demand. It is not clear yet whether geographical diversification of production activities in this sector, which is occurring in Southeast Asia, will strengthen in the future. However, increased competition in the world textile and clothing market with the phase-out of the MFA would lead region-wide reorganization of production activities amongst AP countries.

The results on apparel exports are similar to those of total textile trade. Again, AP developing economies do not seem to have rapidly responded to the changes in demand structure. The product-mix effects are all negative. However, the South Asian economies show positive signs in the competitiveness factor, although the extent of this factor's contribution to export growth is far below that of the Southeast Asian less-developed economies. This fact could explain why Hong Kong SAR, China manufactures have recently been moving to Vietnam, Laos and Cambodia.

Policy implications for AP countries

Liberalization of trade and investment

With the liberalization of trade and investment, AP developing countries are given the opportunity to rely further on their comparative advantages in natural resources and cheap labour. When opening up domestic markets, countries tend to make a better use of cheap labour and natural resources in response to competition. Therefore, they will strengthen international competitiveness in sectors where they have comparative advantage.

AP developing countries can also attract technology transfers from developed countries and improve corporate management by acquiring advanced technology and managerial skills applicable to high value-added items. As a result, AP developing economies will become more stable and competitive, which will lead to sustainable economic growth. This is a major reason why AP developing countries should push ahead with trade and investment liberalization. This calls for the adoption of the following policies:

1. They should *actively react and adjust to the multilateral trading system.* Under the existing system, in which some advanced countries such as the US, EU, Japan and Canada have led the world economy, the AP developing countries have responded to the system in a passive and inactive way. However, with China's entry to the WTO, AP developing countries will be enticed to engage more actively in the multilateral trading system. In doing so, rather than negatively responding to trade and investment liberalization, they need to come up with better schemes to improve their position. In addition, they will have to comply with the international norms related to trade and investment liberalization.

2. They should *actively* participate *in regional economic cooperation programmes* which are designed to promote trade and investment liber-

alization. As is well known, regional trade agreements have recently been increasing in number. According to the WTO, trade agreements within General Agreement on Tariff and Trade (GATT)/WTO totalled 107 as of April 1999. Among them, 77 new regional agreements (72 per cent of the total) were made during the nine years since 1990. Assuming that the number of agreements not yet reported to the GATT/WTO exceeds 100, it is clear that regionalism tends to become fairly universal.

In the past, free-trade agreements were made mainly either among developed or among AP developing countries. In recent years, however, free-trade agreements between developed and AP developing countries are prevailing. Thus, it seems that the stage of development is not a key consideration in reaching such agreements. While there is controversy over the relationship between regionalism and multilateralism, the consensus is growing that regionalism is not necessarily detrimental, but can be complementary to multilateralism in achieving trade liberalization. Regional trade agreements usually contain higher levels of obligations to liberalize than the multilateral ones. This allows the pursuit of more advanced liberalization schemes among smaller numbers of nations.

3. *Bilateral investment treaties* (BIT) are also worth pursuing for similar reasons; they can help the AP developing countries attract foreign investment and adopt technology from developed countries in a more stable environment. With China's entry to the WTO, developed countries may wish to contract FTAs or BITs with China's neighbours in order not only to make use of their cheap labour and natural resources, but also to penetrate more aggressively into the Chinese market in the future. AP developing countries need to take this opportunity to attract foreign capital and advanced technology.

4. It should be emphasized that *domestic regulatory reform* is one of fundamental and necessary conditions for trade and investment liberalization. AP developing countries should make domestic regulations consistent with international norms; they have to realize that liberalization is to ensure not only better market access but also fair competition between domestic and foreign competitors. They can pursue trade and investment liberalization successfully by complying with international norms and ensuring transparency in domestic institutions.

Response to new trade issues

It is very difficult to predict exactly when the new trade issues will be effectively incorporated into the multilateral trade agenda. Despite progress made up to Doha, much remains to be done at the WTO to reach an agreement on those issues. The most immediate priority is to narrow down the differences in the views on new trade issues between developed and AP developing countries. Even though multilateral rules on the new trade issues are expected to contribute to enhancing the world economic and social welfare in the long run, they may have negative economic impacts on the AP developing countries in the short run.

First of all, the strengthening of environmental disciplines will raise the production costs of firms requiring a substantial change in production processes and technology. Furthermore, part of those costs may be transferred to consumers, raising the consumer price as well. Similar effects are expected in relation to the issue of labour standards. Upward adjustment of labour standards may cause shortages in labour supply, raising labor costs. Ensuring the core labour standards may induce higher wages through enforcement of the workers' collective bargaining status *vis-à-vis* employers.[12]

Multilateral rules of competition policy and transparency in government procurement related with anti-corruption are also difficult for AP developing countries to accept, at least in the short run, when their domestic systems and practices are considered. Not many AP developing countries have yet adopted competition policies in their domestic economies. Much opaqueness remains in their businesses as well as in their public sectors. Reforming systems and practices in those areas will certainly cause huge social as well as economic adjustment costs. Even liberalization in investment will be a very difficult task for some AP developing countries. They want to selectively open areas of foreign investment that are consistent with their development strategies. Protection for certain domestic industries may be another reason why they are unwilling to liberalize investment.

Considering all of these, developed countries should give sufficient time for AP developing countries to adapt to the new trade issues and assist them with relevant technology and know-how. AP developing countries, in exchange, should prepare to take measures and implement them.

AP developing countries should expand investment in protection of the environment. It is obvious that the issue will become more important as overseas sales of commodities not meeting environmental standards are not permitted. They should adopt preventive environment policies and assist domestic firms to the greatest extent in building up environment-friendly workplaces. The government should set up rules or administrative guidelines to implement, even if they are granted a grace period.

International norms on labour issues will take some time to agree upon, because AP developing countries still strongly resist them. However, it may be possible that a minimum level of guidelines for labour standards could be set up through the International Labour Organization (ILO), based upon careful research results. AP developing countries should take more progressive action on labour issues in order to continue to be able to export commodities where they have comparative advantages. It should be admitted that adjustment to international labour standards would lead to higher productivity, better quality control and export competitiveness.

It is also likely that international norms will be adopted in the areas of competition policy, anti-corruption and corporate governance. This is certainly no easy task for developing countries, but they may not be able to address it because these areas are directly interlinked with nations' self-images. Since those issues are highly co-related with globalization, developed countries will not give them up easily either. China is a good example in this matter.

Industrial restructuring

As the world economy becomes globalized and the Chinese economy is integrated into the multilateral trading system, AP developing countries may experience many difficulties in the short run. Their economies will stagnate in poverty unless they can overcome problems of lack of industrial technology, oversupply of labour, inconsistencies with international norms, and inefficiencies in economic management. In order to resolve those problems, they have to pursue dramatic industrial restructuring. In principle, they have to strengthen export competitiveness, building up knowledge-based industries. Technology should be developed to improve non-price competitiveness.

In many areas, China's major exports compete with those of developing countries. This competition can cause a problem for developing countries, not only in their exports to China or to developed countries, but also in their domestic markets. Their major exports, such as agricultural products, textiles, raw materials and cheap manufacturing commodities, are already price-competitive. So are Chinese products. Unless the AP developing countries improve competitiveness in non-price factors such as quality, function, design, packaging and the like, their export markets will be rapidly encroached upon by Chinese products. That is why AP developing countries should promote industrial restructuring and build up knowledge-based industries, as well as:

- Establish knowledge-based industry structures, first by utilizing their conventional industries, and then by moving towards industries with higher technology
- Develop service industries, without which they cannot achieve international competitiveness
- Make great efforts to build up environment-friendly domestic industries, as a matter of competitive survival
- Enforce an effective competition policy, in particular to allow small- and medium-sized enterprises to enjoy fair market conditions
- Reform the public sector to avoid capture by vested interests and achieve efficient management
- Set-up effective industrial support systems to develop dynamic comparative advantages
- Expand investment in education so that the labour force can move to higher-value activities. This effort should include enhancing managerial skills

Notes

1 Lu (2000), p. 9.
2 Those outlines were approved at the fourth session of China's 8th National People's Congress in March 1996.
3 Lu (2000), p. 6.
4 And with the EU on 19 May 2000.
5 Within three years from the accession, foreign service suppliers may establish wholly-owned subsidiaries.
6 The chief representative of a foreign law firm must be a partner or equivalent in a law firm from a WTO member country. All representatives must be a member of the bar in a WTO member country, possess three years' experience outside of China, and reside in China no less than six months each year.
7 Yoo (1999); Rosen (1999).
8 Whalley (1994).
9 Elasticities for each product are calculated from dividing changes of import value by changes in trade-weighted tariffs between 1995 and 1998. We divided the elasticities by two to remove income effects on the import expansion during this period. So the effects from the tariff reduction are subject to relative importance of price and income effects on imports.

10 The US negotiated safeguard is available upon China's accession to the WTO until 2008, four years after the last quotas are set to be lifted by importing countries under the ATC. This will give some time for other developing economies to enhance their competitiveness.

11 USITC (1999).

12 The relationship between labour standards and trade has been examined by Rodrik (1996). The study shows that lax labour standards are highly associated with lower costs in a cross-section of countries.

References and bibliography

Barfield, C. E. (1999), 'The China WTO deal: sweet and sour', *The Asian Wall Street Journal*, 17 November.

Chae, W. (2000), 'The world trade environment in the new century', *The New World Economic Order in the 21st Century*, Seminar Paper, Korea Institute for International Economic Policy.

Goad, G. P. (1999), 'Asia's gains and losses', *Far Eastern Economic Review*, 25 November.

IMF (2000), *World Economic Outlook*.

Kim, I. (1999), *China's Accession into WTO and its Multi-Faced Impact on East Asia and the Korean Economy*, Policy Analysis 99-09, Korea Institute for International Economic Policy.

Lardy, N. (1999), 'China's WTO membership', *The Brookings Policy Brief*. No 47, Brokings Institution.

Lawrence, S. V. (1999), 'Deal of the century', *Far Eastern Economic Review*, 25 November.

Lu, D. (2000), 'Industrial policy and China's participation in globalization', *China–Korea Economic Forum 2000*, Korea Institute for International Economic Policy.

OECD (1997), *Towards a New Global Age: Challenges and Opportunities*, Draft Analytical Report, OECD.

Rodrik, D. (1996), 'Labour standards and international trade: do they matter and what do we do about them?', in R. Lawrence et al., *Emerging Agenda for Global Trade: High Stakes for Developing Countries* (Overseas Development Council, Washington DC).

Rosen, D. H. (1999), 'China and the WTO: an economic balance sheet', *International Economic Policy Briefs*, Institute for International Economies.

UNCTAD (2000), *Trade Information System* (TRAINS).

USITC (1999), 'Impacts on the US economy of China's accession to the WTO'.

USTR (1999a), 'US China Sign Historic Trade Agreement', http://www.ustr.gov/releases/1999/11/99-05.html, 14 December.

—— (1999b), 'USTR Barshefsky's press remarks following negotiations with China on the WTO', 14 December.

Whalley, J. (1994), 'Textile and clothing', paper presented at the OECD Informal Workshop (Paris: OECD).

White House (1999), 'Summary of US–China bilateral WTO agreement,' 15 November.

WTO (2000), *Annual Report 2000*.

Yoo, J. S. (1999), 'China accession to the WTO and its impacts', Issue paper, Samsung Economic Research Institute.

4

The Competitive Impact of China on Manufactured Exports by Emerging Economies in Asia

Sanjaya Lall and Manuel Albaladejo

F14 P33
019 L40

Introduction

China's accession to the World Trade Organization (WTO), with the consequent liberalization of trade and investment, will have significant competitive repercussions on the developing world. Given the size and dynamism of the Chinese economy, these effects will be felt not only in the neighbouring region in Southeast Asia but also across the globe. The impact will have positive and negative aspects, depending on the country and activity concerned. Some countries will gain from the opening up of the Chinese market and from the opportunities offered to invest there, not just for selling locally but also for exporting to other markets. Other countries will be faced with intensified competition in both export and home markets, and may suffer erosion in market share and industrial performance.

Here we will focus on one aspect of China's competitive impact: on *manufactured exports by emerging Asian economies* (exports to the rest of the world, not to China). We also make some reference to other developing countries. The focus on manufactures is understandable. While primary product exports by other countries may also be affected by China's WTO accession, this effect is unlikely to be large. China is not a major exporter of such products and such exports do not in any case raise important analytical issues. They depend largely on the availability of exportable natural resources rather than on the development of new competitive advantages.[1]

Manufactured exports, on the other hand, do raise important and complex issues. They reflect the interaction of several types of competitive advantage – many of them subject to policy influence. Manufactures are much more dynamic than primary exports (Lall, 2001) and have more important development implications, both in terms of the capabilities they require and the learning and spillovers they generate for industry as well as the rest of the economy. For China, they are also far more significant: in 1998, they accounted for 91 per cent of its merchandise exports. China has now emerged as the largest exporter of manufactured products in the developing world. The growth of its manufactured exports has been among the fastest achieved by developing countries, and they are not, as sometimes thought, based only on cheap labour. The exports span a broad range of technologies, so reflecting an impressive range of competitive strengths, and are diversifying and upgrading with amazing rapidity. All this can be seen as a threat to countries both above and below China in terms of industrial development. We shall seek to provide a broad picture of these threats.

It is not possible, however, to explore the competitive implications of China for manufactured exports for emerging Asia in great detail. This would require extensive analysis at the level of specific industries and countries, beyond the scope of this chapter. Our objective here is to provide a broad-brush picture of recent export performance and to infer from patterns of manufactured exports of China and Asian countries where the main competitive challenges are likely to arise.[2]

Analytical framework

The net competitive impact of the 'opening-up' of a very large and dynamic economy on its neighbours is a complex mixture of costs and benefits, depending on the activity, country and relative growth of the capabilities that determine competitiveness. Consider a simple scheme, with two main sorts of costs (competitive threats) and benefits (competitive opportunities). The main potential *competitive threats* are:

1. *More intense competition in export markets.* China is already a strong international competitor in a large range of industrial products, led by simple labour-intensive manufactures but rapidly diversifying into complex, capital and technology-intensive goods (see below). WTO accession will strengthen its competitive position across the range. While accession may not give China an immediate advantage in markets where it already enjoys most-favoured-nation (MFN) status (see Chapter 3), it will give it freer access to other markets. Just as

important, accession will assure it secure access in the future, and so induce more sustained investment in building exports. Entry into the WTO will also accompany other forms of trade liberalization, the most important being the removal of MFA restrictions on textiles and garments by the end of 2004. This will strengthen China's position in several products of export significance to other countries. Liberalization will also induce technological upgrading in many activities, and the accompanying improvement in the business climate will make China a more attractive location for foreign direct investment (FDI).

There are two sources of the competitive threat to other countries: domestic firms and affiliates of transnational corporations (TNCs). Both are likely to improve and enlarge their export profile in China after liberalization. *Domestic firms* are major and growing industrial exporters, accounting for over half of Chinese manufactured exports.[3] They are likely to undergo significant restructuring after trade and investment liberalization (Zhang, 2000). The ones that survive will emerge as keener global competitors, based in a huge domestic market and a strong supporting industrial structure. They will enter a larger range of industrial activities, using not only low-cost labour but a range of other competitive assets and skills that are being improved over time.

Export-oriented FDI has been the main force behind China's manufactured export growth. The growth of such exports is likely to continue after WTO accession. TNCs seeking competitive production sites will be attracted to the more liberal, stable and transparent investment environment and growing capabilities in China. The main draw will still be in low technology, labour-intensive assembly activity, but there is likely to be a rising share of complex, technology-intensive activities, possibly with growing local content. A significant part of such FDI will continue to come from the mature 'Tiger' economies in East Asia,[4] but it is likely that an increasing part will come from mature industrial countries. This can be a competitive threat to other developing economies in the region (and further afield) that base their export and industrial growth on FDI, and that specialize in the same product and market segments. It can also be a threat to the Tigers that invest in China, if their own industries that are relocating ('hollowing out') fail to develop new competitive capabilities sufficiently to sustain high rates of domestic growth.

2. *More intense competition in domestic markets.* Many emerging Asian economies (and those in other regions) still have significant protection

against imports from other developing countries. As they open their markets up in line with WTO rules, they will face intensifying competition from China. The activities involved will be the same as those in exports to the rest of the world, starting with simple industries like textiles, apparel, footwear or toys, and going on to more capital- and technology-intensive industries.

Chinese liberalization also offers *competitive opportunities* to developing countries:

(a) *Selling to and producing in China.* As the Chinese economy opens up to foreign goods, services and FDI, other countries will benefit from the vast and dynamic market both by exporting from home and by setting up facilities locally. The extent to which they tap such opportunities depends on their competitive strengths relative to Chinese counterparts.

(b) *Relocating export-oriented facilities to China.* Countries with relatively high wages and strong competitive advantages (the mature Tigers) will, as noted, continue to invest in China to export to the rest of the world. *Export*-oriented activity will probably spread from the Special Economic Zones (SEZs) to other regions as wages rise in the SEZs and infrastructure improves elsewhere. The benefit of 'hollowing out' is that it helps investing countries to sustain existing competitive advantages for longer periods and helps restructure domestic industry into higher-value functions (design, marketing or research and development (R&D)) and more advanced activities. The extent to which this promotes growth depends on the rate at which domestic capabilities are generated relative to the rate at which activities are relocated.

3. *Finding new niches in integrated international production systems.* A similar restructuring process may also apply to countries (like Malaysia, Thailand or Philippines in the region) that depend on foreign investors to drive their export effort. While labour-intensive segments of TNC activities may be increasingly placed in China, TNCs may invest in these other countries in more complex functions and products. This is already happening in some industries. For instance, a regional triangle has emerged in the hard disk drive industry, with the most advanced activities located in Singapore, the intermediate levels in Thailand and the lower levels in China (Doner and Brimble, 1998). China is, however, continuously pushing to upgrade its role in integrated production

systems, challenging countries in the segments immediately above it. The ability of these other countries to keep ahead depends, again, on their ability to provide cheaper and better capabilities (skills, suppliers, support institutions and infrastructure) than offered by China.[5]

The net competitive impact of China will therefore vary by country, industry, function and time. It will comprise complicated interactions between competitive and complementary forces, often co-existing in the same industry or even firm. China may, for example, compete fiercely with the Bangladeshi apparel industry for a time and then decide to relocate some facilities there to take advantage of lower wages. Or it may undertake lower-value functions in an integrated TNC system for a while before moving up the technology ladder to draw more advanced activities away from its former collaborators. It may move into the economies of more advanced countries in a region such as the Republic of Korea and Taiwan Province of China, buying up innovating firms and transferring the source of competitive advantage (this was the strategy pursued by many Korean and Taiwanese electronics firms in the US). Whether the final effect is complementary or competitive depends ultimately on the relative rate at which the different countries enhance their competitive capabilities.

In such a dynamic and variegated setting, therefore, it is impossible to predict the competitive impact with any degree of confidence. Only detailed industry or firm-level studies can provide answers, and even these may be of limited reliability and duration. The available evidence only permits an assessment of the general directions of the competitive challenge posed by China. It does not allow us to make even rough quantitative estimates. As noted, we focus on competition in *export markets*, that is excluding competition in domestic markets in China and comparators. However, to the extent that the determinants of competitive performance in each other's markets are similar to those in competitiveness in export markets, there are some useful insights here.

The assessment of China's competitive impact takes place in two stages. In the first, we compare the industrial and manufactured export structures in China and other economies by levels of technology. It is assumed that the more similar the structures in technological terms, the more intense is competition likely to be. This analysis has limitations. The technological classification is fairly simple and aggregate[6]; the level at which comparable data are readily available forces us to lump together some diverse activities. Thus, the analysis ignores the potential for specialization within broad categories (which may lead to complementarity rather than to competition). It also ignores the possibility that countries may complement each other even within narrow categories, even in a single given export product, if they undertake different processes within integrated TNC systems. The data at hand do not allow for such refinements. On the other hand, the technological categorization does capture a critical aspect of industrial competitiveness, one that is of increasing importance – the role of technologically advanced products, which are steadily raising their shares of world trade and production (UNIDO, 2002).

The purpose of technological classification is more than convenience: there is an analytical underpinning. More technology-intensive activities and exports may be considered relatively desirable for export competitiveness, for two reasons. First, complex activities are growing more rapidly in trade than simple activities (Figure 4.1). Primary products and RB manufactures are steadily losing shares in world trade. High-technology products are the most dynamic element in world trade, and have raised their shares in total manufactured exports from 12 per cent in 1985 to 21 per cent in 1998; on the basis of recent performance they will soon account for the largest single share.

MT products, the largest category (33 per cent in 1998) grew slightly slower than LT products in 1985–90 but faster since 1990. In the long term, given the underlying technological trends, MT products are likely to grow faster than LT products. The latter's growth is driven by a shift in production location from high- to low-wage countries, with demand growing slowly and product innovation weak. MT export growth is more dependent, as with HT, on innovation and high-income elastic-

Figure 4.1 Rates of growth of world exports by technology categories

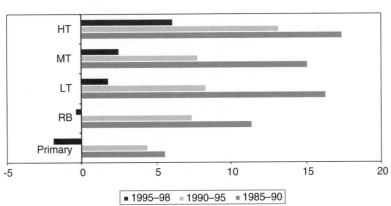

ity of demand. Thus, structural factors (technical progress and rising incomes) will favour the faster growth of complex products. Market 'positioning' requires that dynamic exporters move up the technology scale.

The other reason why complex exports are better for competitiveness is that they often offer greater learning and spillover benefits (Lall, 2001). The capabilities created by sophisticated industrial activities are deeper and more advanced than those created by low-technology activities and so are more conducive to industrial development. Deeper learning is necessary to sustain competitiveness as wages rise: specialization at the low end of simple export activities can only be maintained by keeping wages and other costs low. Dynamic comparative advantage necessarily involves going up the technology ladder, even for developing countries. Sophisticated export activities also tend to generate more externalities and have greater applicability to other industries. One reason for the export success (along with wage growth) in East Asia has been the rapid move from simple to complex export products. In fact, countries like Republic of Korea and Taiwan Province of China, and later Thailand and Malaysia, are relocating low-technology export activities to lower-wage countries while expanding in high-technology ones.

The next stage of the competitiveness assessment is to compare 'industrial capabilities' – the structural drivers of export competitiveness – across countries. There are again limitations we should note at the start. The choice of variables here is, however, limited by data availability, and the measures of the variables included are far from perfect. We exclude factors in national competitiveness that cannot be quantified, like the quality of institutions, business transaction costs, the quality of labour, the impact of taxes and subsidies and so on. We cover the following: wage rates, skill levels, technological effort, inward FDI, technology imports in other forms and modern information and communications technology (ICT) infrastructure. However, as discussed later, the measures are often rough proxies. Nevertheless, they do capture important features of the competitive structure, and are highly correlated with industrial performance (UNIDO, 2002).

The comparators in Southeast Asia are the four mature Tigers (Hong Kong SAR, China, Singapore, Republic of Korea and Taiwan Province of China) and the four new Tigers (Indonesia, Malaysia, Philippines and Thailand). In South Asia they are India, Pakistan, Bangladesh and Sri Lanka. We also include the three largest Latin American economies

(Argentina, Brazil and Mexico) and Sub-Saharan Africa (SSA) (including South Africa).

Comparing industrial and export structures

Manufacturing production

The first striking thing about comparing manufacturing industry in China and other developing economies is the sheer difference in size. As Table 4.1 shows, manufacturing value added (MVA) in China in 1990 was approximately half that in the rest of Southeast Asia combined; it is now slightly larger. In the 1990s, the Chinese growth rate is

Table 4.1 Manufacturing value added (constant US$ million)

	1990	*1999*	*(2003 projection)*	*Growth rate percentage (90–99)*
China	117 033	375 997	631 630	13.8
Thailand	23 043	39 798	50 739	6.3
Malaysia	10 566	25 292	37 280	10.2
Indonesia	24 030	35 628	42 443	4.5
Philippines	11 083	16 077	18 968	4.2
New Tigers	**68 721**	**116 796**	**149 430**	**5.8**
Hong Kong SAR, China	13 461	9 537	8 182	–3.8
Rep of Korea	73 260	130 221	168 154	6.6
Singapore	9 892	22 086	31 560	9.3
Taiwan Prov.*	53 522	75 772	88 432	3.9
Mature Tigers	**150 136**	**237 615**	**296 328**	**5.2**
E. Asia excl. China	**218 857**	**354 411**	**445 758**	**5.4**
Bangladesh	3 917	6 894	8 864	6.5
India	53 756	71 567	81 274	3.2
Pakistan	6 802	9 305	10 695	3.5
Sri Lanka	1 205	2 553	3 565	8.7
South Asia	**65 679**	**90 319**	**104 397**	**4.3**
Argentina	38 165	50 970	57 964	3.3
Brazil	116 247	172 846	206 171	4.5
Mexico	55 169	101 585	133 249	7.0
Latin America	**209 581**	**325 401**	**397 384**	**4.5**
SSA	**50 565**	**51 856**	**52 439**	**0.3**

* Data from Taiwan Statistical Data Book, various issues.
Regional subtotals are for the countries shown in the table.
Projected MVA is based on growth rates for 1990–99 for each country. The regional subtotal for 2003 is not calculated from the regional growth rate but is the sum for the projected country figures.
Source: Calculated from World Bank, *World Development Indicators 2001*.

2.6 times higher than in the region, which is itself the most dynamic part of the world economy. MVA in the other giant economy in Asia, India, was 46 per cent of China's in 1990; it is now a mere 13 per cent. The three Latin American economies combined produce less than 60 per cent of China. The whole of SSA, including South Africa (which in turn accounts for nearly 60 per cent of the regional total), produces about 8 per cent. If we project MVA on the basis of recent growth rates, by 2003 China will be larger than East Asia, South Asia and Sub-Saharan Africa *combined*. Of course, such simple projections are only illustrative – future performance may differ greatly from the past.

China is not just the largest industrial economy in the developing world it is also the fastest growing. This combination may have significant implications for its competitiveness. *Large size* implies the ability to realize scale and scope economies, and so export products that are more difficult for smaller economies to provide. The latter can set up large-scale facilities solely for export markets (for example, Singapore in petrochemicals), but this is more risky and does not allow a cushion for building local technological capabilities. It has to be handled by TNCs rather than by local firms, which may restrict local linkages, spillovers and diversification. China can, by contrast, launch relatively capital-intensive and complex activities within local firms and gain export competence by learning in the domestic market. The additional advantage this provides is the associated learning and linkage benefits that entry into complex industries provides. Furthermore, thanks to the large size of the domestic market, export activities can have far higher local content, including those in scale-intensive provide intermediate and capital goods. Apart from the benefits just noted, having local supply sources can be an additional source of competitive edge for exporters. It can provide greater flexibil-ity in designing and sourcing inputs, developing new technologies and diversifying into related activities. Suppliers to exporters in turn can benefit from their clients' exposure to world markets and technologies. These dynamic benefits are more truncated for smaller economies.

The relatively *rapid growth* of Chinese industry is likely to comple-ment its size advantages. It means that its enterprises are investing in newer equipment and technology than its competitors. Fast growth is often associated with rapid productivity growth (enterprises introduce new management methods and skills, in addition to new equipment). It facilitates industrial restructuring, from slow growing to dynamic products. It may also have less tangible benefits, like encouraging risk taking and investment more generally, and stimulating the growth of supporting services and institutions. The extent to which this potential has been realized in China cannot, of course, be judged from the available data. However, WTO accession is likely to strengthen such advantages in China, as infrastructure and services are opened up to foreign entry and industry leaders are attracted to the giant, growing market.

Table 4.2 shows the evolution of the *technological structure of MVA* in China and comparators. Data problems do not allow us to distinguish between medium and high technology activities, and the two are taken together as 'complex' activities. These account for just over half of Chinese MVA in 1997. This is higher than in the New Tigers (except for Malaysia, with its large export-oriented electronics industry), but lower than in the mature Tigers, India and Brazil (the last two with long legacies, like China, of heavy import substitution). In the industrial world, the share of medium and high technology (MHT) in MVA is around 60 per cent. In global terms, the Chinese structure is at an

Table 4.2   Technological structure of MVA (%)

	1985			1997		
	MHT	*LT*	*RB*	*MHT*	*LT*	*RB*
China	**49.1**	**20.8**	**30.1**	**50.9**	**17.9**	**31.2**
Thailand	17.8	30.3	51.9	38.6	24.5	36.8
Malaysia	46.9	9.8	43.3	60.1	11.4	28.5
Indonesia	25.2	14.6	60.2	40.3	24.8	34.8
Philippines	22.4	9.7	67.9	36.3	10.9	52.8
New Tigers	**28.1**	**16.1**	**55.8**	**43.8**	**17.9**	**38.2**
Hong Kong SAR	38.3	51.9	9.8	52.5	30.2	17.3
Rep of Korea	46.6	23.5	29.9	60.5	16.8	22.7
Singapore	66.9	12.6	20.5	79.9	8.1	12.0
Taiwan Prov.	43.1	28.3	28.5	56.5	18.5	25.0
Mature Tigers	**48.7**	**29.1**	**22.2**	**62.4**	**18.4**	**19.3**
E. Asia exc. China	**38.4**	**22.6**	**39.0**	**53.1**	**18.2**	**28.7**
Bangladesh	28.3	33.2	38.4	28.0	41.9	30.1
India	55.6	18.9	25.5	59.0	16.0	24.9
Pakistan	36.3	20.8	42.8	34.4	26.7	38.9
Sri Lanka	10.2	26.3	63.5	15.6	43.5	40.8
S. Asia	**32.6**	**24.8**	**42.6**	**34.3**	**32.0**	**33.7**
Argentina	34.0	16.9	49.1	37.1	18.5	44.4
Brazil	54.1	19.0	26.9	57.9	13.0	29.1
Mexico	36.8	19.0	44.2	35.6	18.1	46.3
L. America	**41.6**	**18.3**	**40.1**	**43.5**	**16.5**	**39.9**
SSA	**38.6**	**18.7**	**42.7**	**37.6**	**18.8**	**43.6**

Note: Regional subtotals are only for the countries shown.
Source: UNIDO (2002).

intermediate level for a country with a large industrial sector, and relatively advanced for one with its (low) income level.[7]

The Chinese industrial structure has been relatively slow to upgrade despite its rapid growth, particularly in comparison with most Asian Tigers. In the latter, the upgrading has been largely driven by export activities, but with different agents involved. In Republic of Korea and Taiwan Province of China, the lead agents have been domestic firms, with a variety of technological and marketing arrangements with foreign companies. In the others, they were mainly TNCs. In both groups, high technology export growth has been mainly the result of participation in integrated production systems, either as independent original equipment manufacture (OEM) producers and subcontractors or as affiliates of TNCs. However, in Republic of Korea and Taiwan Province of China (and to a small extent, in Singapore), local high-tech firms have also developed sufficient independent capabilities to set up their own global production chains.

This is not the case with the other countries, where technology-intensive exports still have low local linkages and technology content. In China, both means of expanding technology-intensive exports have been used with impressive results (see below). However, given the size of its industrial sector, this does not yet show up in the Chinese MVA structure; the upgrading of the export structure thus outpaces that of the MVA structure.

The implications for China's competitive challenge are mixed. On the one hand, the size and growth of the industrial sector imply a large threat, once it fully 'comes on stream' in world markets. On the other hand, the slow upgrading of MVA suggests that considerable restructuring is needed before a threat is posed to more advanced export activities. At present, the main threat may be concentrated in simpler manufacturing activities: of these, RB products are likely to be less affected than LT, where China has an edge in a massive industrial base, cheap labour and established marketing links. The effects are likely to be felt in labour-intensive exports both in the region and afield (in South Asia, North Africa, Caribbean and so on). In the longer term, there is also a threat to less industrialized countries (for example, in Africa) that are not significant exporters of manufactures but hope to export labour-intensive products in the future. They would need a large wage advantage over China to compensate for their smaller base of industrial capabilities and production base. However, China's challenge in complex exports should not be discounted on the basis of the above figures. As shown below, China is now a dynamic and substantial exporter of high-tech products, far more than its MVA upgrading suggests. It has been able to reorient parts of its inherited structure and add new export-oriented segments successfully, far more effectively than other large, formerly import-substituting countries (Mexico is the other success, thanks to North American Free Trade Association (NAFTA)). Its SEZs are similar in competitiveness and dynamism to those in the Tiger economies, with the added advantage of lower wages and a strong 'Chinese connection' with other export-oriented economies. On top of this, they have behind them the giant market and a massive and dense industrial base – these may not have mattered greatly for some exports till now, but over time are bound to matter more. Much will depend on how quickly China is able to build upon its initial success by enhancing its capabilities – this is dealt with in further below.

Manufactured export performance: broad categories

We start with overall export performance. Table 4.3 shows data on total manufactured exports for 1985-98, with projections for 2003 based on past growth rates (note again that such projections are not predictions). China is by far the largest exporter of manufactures in the developing world, but its lead is much smaller than for MVA – not surprisingly in view of its legacy of isolation and its recent entry into world markets. Given this background, however, its export dynamism is impressive. Driven by assembly operations by foreign affiliates, joint ventures and local firms, its connections with Chinese communities in Hong Kong SAR, China and Taiwan Province of China, and its locational advantages with respect to the Republic of Korea and Japan, its manufactured exports grew at nearly 30 per cent per annum in this period.

This is much faster than the most dynamic Tigers in Asia (or Mexico, the most dynamic large exporter in other regions). In 1998 China accounted for 17 per cent of total manufactured exports by developing countries, up from 3.1 per cent in 1985. It was the world's seventh largest exporter of manufactures, and may rank higher today.

While these data indicate China's competitive strengths, it is useful to look beyond the aggregate figures at the technological composition of exports. There is a widespread impression that China's main competitive strength lies in labour-intensive, low-technology products. China certainly dominates world markets in many labour-intensive exports, and its relatively cheap and productive labour force gives it a clear advantage. However, if its competitive edge were confined to cheap

Table 4.3 Total manufactured exports (current US$ million)

	1985	1998	2003 (projection)	Growth rate (85–98)
China	6 049	167 681	601 732	29.1
Thailand	3 658	44 760	117 281	21.2
Malaysia	8 626	65 941	144 175	16.9
Indonesia	3 856	26 895	56 766	16.1
Philippines	2 429	28 119	72 125	20.7
New Tigers	18 569	165 714	390 347	18.3
Hong Kong SAR, China (1)	15 979	23 137	26 676	2.9
Rep of Korea	29 025	120 700	208 814	11.6
Singapore (1)	19 014	103 489	198 563	13.9
Taiwan Prov. (2)	29 092	105 554	173 277	10.4
Mature Tigers	93 111	352 879	607 331	10.8
E. Asia exc. China	111 680	518 593	997 678	12.5
Bangladesh	793	4 691	9 293	14.6
India	6 209	25 855	44 754	11.6
Pakistan	1 776	7 428	12 880	11.6
Sri Lanka	582	3 043	5 750	13.6
S. Asia	9 360	41 018	72 677	12.0
Argentina	3 703	14 108	23 599	10.8
Brazil	17 617	38 882	52 721	6.3
Mexico	8 336	103 681	273 370	21.4
L. America	29 656	156 671	349 689	13.7
SSA	7 172	18 592	26 818	7.6

Notes: Regional sub-totals are only for countries shown.
(1) Data exclude re-exports.
(2) Data from Taiwan Province of China Statistical Data Book, various issues.
Source: Calculated from UN Comtrade database.

efficient labour, its competitive challenge would be relatively limited. It would not affect greatly countries with advantages in more complex products. The advantage would, moreover, erode quickly as Chinese incomes rose. Rapid technical progress and changing market conditions would also threaten such a static source of comparative advantage: sustained export dynamism needs upgrading into advanced technologies within activities and from simple to sophisticated activities.

Upgrading is just what China is doing. While exploiting its advantage in low-cost labour, it is moving up the technology ladder within and across products. It is difficult to capture upgrading within product categories with the available data. What is possible to quantify is changes in the technological structure of exports across categories.

Let us look at the distribution and growth of manufactured exports by technology (Table 4.4). In 1985, LT and RB products (83 per cent)

Table 4.4 Technological structure of manufactured exports and growth rates (%)

	1985				1998				Annual growth rates (85–98)			
	HT	MT	LT	RB	HT	MT	LT	RB	HT	MT	LT	RB
China	**5.2**	**12.2**	**43.7**	**38.8**	**20.0**	**20.2**	**50.0**	**9.9**	**43.2**	**34.2**	**30.5**	**16.2**
Thailand	4.7	22.0	35.4	37.9	34.8	20.5	25.3	19.3	41.4	20.6	18.2	15.1
Malaysia	26.9	11.4	8.0	53.7	52.1	20.3	11.0	16.7	23.0	22.2	19.8	6.9
Indonesia	3.0	6.4	15.5	75.2	9.7	18.5	33.0	38.8	27.2	26.0	23.1	10.4
Philippines	11.0	9.0	24.1	56.0	67.4	10.9	14.5	7.2	38.8	22.5	16.1	3.1
New Tigers	**10.2**	**12.2**	**25.3**	**52.3**	**36.8**	**18.1**	**26.8**	**18.4**	**28.0**	**22.2**	**19.3**	**9.2**
Hong Kong SAR	14.8	19.1	63.0	3.2	26.0	13.2	56.3	4.5	7.5	0.0	2.0	5.7
Rep of Korea	12.8	37.2	41.4	8.6	29.8	38.5	21.0	10.7	19.1	11.9	5.9	13.5
Singapore	24.5	23.4	8.6	43.5	60.2	18.7	7.0	14.1	22.1	12.0	12.1	4.5
Taiwan Prov.	16.2	21.1	52.9	9.9	36.6	27.5	30.4	5.5	17.6	12.7	5.8	5.5
Mature Tigers	**17.1**	**25.2**	**41.5**	**16.3**	**38.2**	**24.5**	**28.7**	**8.7**	**18.7**	**11.3**	**5.4**	**7.1**
E. Asia exc. China	**13.6**	**18.7**	**33.4**	**34.3**	**37.5**	**21.3**	**27.7**	**13.5**	**20.8**	**12.8**	**7.6**	**8.0**
Bangladesh	0.2	2.0	77.6	20.3	0.3	2.8	94.2	2.7	17.2	18.0	16.4	-1.9
India	4.1	10.1	45.3	40.6	6.6	14.6	48.7	30.2	15.8	14.8	12.2	9.1
Pakistan	0.3	11.9	81.6	6.3	0.7	9.7	84.5	5.1	20.7	9.9	11.9	9.8
Sri Lanka	0.4	2.6	55.2	41.8	1.9	3.3	77.5	17.3	29.2	15.5	16.6	6.1
S. Asia	**1.2**	**6.6**	**64.9**	**27.2**	**2.4**	**7.6**	**76.2**	**13.8**	**16.2**	**13.9**	**13.1**	**8.6**
Argentina	4.4	19.0	16.3	60.2	4.6	37.3	14.4	43.7	11.1	16.7	9.8	8.1
Brazil	4.9	29.8	21.3	44.0	8.2	36.9	15.2	39.7	10.6	8.1	3.5	5.4
Mexico	22.5	43.2	13.2	21.1	30.1	44.0	19.1	6.7	24.2	21.6	24.9	11.2
L. America	**10.6**	**30.7**	**16.9**	**41.8**	**14.3**	**39.4**	**16.2**	**30.0**	**21.1**	**15.9**	**13.3**	**7.1**
SSA	6.6	18.2	17.3	57.9	5.3	25.5	23.3	45.8	5.8	10.4	10.1	5.7

Note: See Table 4.3.
Source: Calculated from the UN Comtrade database

dominated Chinese exports. Only South Asia had a more LT/RB dependent structure at the time. HT products provided only 5 per cent of Chinese exports, about the level of Thailand, Indonesia, India, Argentina, Brazil and Africa (including South Africa). By 1998, the share of MHT had risen to 40 per cent for China; that of RB had declined dramatically while that of LT had grown. China had pulled far ahead of South Asia in terms of technological complexity; the latter had practically stagnated in complex exports while significantly raising the LT share (at the expense of RB). Latin America had raised its technological complexity, largely because of Mexico's surge in HT products and the growth of MT exports from Argentina and Brazil. However, the region remains highly dependent on RB, with its HT profile lagging well behind East Asia. The export structures of the Asian Tigers are generally more advanced than of China. In particular, the share of HT products is higher in all countries except Indonesia. China shows a massive increase in LT products, with a compound growth rate of 31 per cent. It is now by far the largest exporter of such products in the developing world (Table 4.5), larger even than the mature Tigers taken together. In fact, a significant portion of China's LT exports come from facilities relocated there by Hong Kong SAR, China, the Republic of Korea and Taiwan Province of China. The new Tigers start the period with a higher market share in LT than China, but China's share rises 3.5 times faster over the period. This confirms Chinese edge in labour-intensive activity. The remainder of the developing world does not even approach half of China's LT market share.

While this confirms Chinese advantages in labour-intensive exports, the rapid growth of more complex exports shows a massive shift into sophisticated products. Most developing regions (apart from Africa) also expand complex exports faster than LT or RB exports, and within complex products HT generally leads MT products.[8] However, it is the *pace* of growth by China that is startling: 43.2 per cent for HT and 34.2 per cent for MT products. Its world market share in HT is now larger than all the countries in the table with the exception of Malaysia, Singapore, Republic of Korea and Taiwan Province of China, all much longer-established HT exporters. At present rates, it will soon overtake all of them except for Singapore (and may already have done this by the time this book is published). In fact, if recent growth rates hold, by 2003 China will be exporting US$201 billion of HT products, compared to US$168 billion for Singapore, US$86 billion each for Republic of Korea and Taiwan Province of China, and US$96 billion for Malaysia. This would take China's world market share in HT exports to

Table 4.5   World market shares of manufactured exports by technological categories

	1985					1998				
	Total	*HT*	*MT*	*LT*	*RB*	*Total*	*HT*	*MT*	*LT*	*RB*
China	**0.5**	**0.1**	**0.1**	**1.1**	**0.8**	**3.9**	**3.1**	**2.0**	**10.4**	**2.2**
Thailand	0.3	0.1	0.2	0.5	0.5	1.0	1.5	0.6	1.4	1.2
Malaysia	0.7	1.1	0.2	0.3	1.5	1.5	3.2	0.8	0.9	1.5
Indonesia	0.3	0.1	0.0	0.2	1.0	0.6	0.2	0.3	1.1	1.4
Philippines	0.2	0.1	0.0	0.2	0.4	0.7	1.8	0.2	0.5	0.3
New Tigers	**1.4**	**1.3**	**0.4**	**1.3**	**3.4**	**3.9**	**6.7**	**1.8**	**3.9**	**4.3**
Hong Kong SAR	1.2	1.1	0.6	4.2	0.2	0.5	0.6	0.2	1.6	0.1
Rep of Korea	2.3	1.7	2.1	5.0	0.8	2.8	3.4	2.8	3.1	1.7
Singapore	1.5	2.2	0.8	0.7	2.7	2.4	5.8	1.2	0.9	2.0
Taiwan Prov.	2.3	2.2	1.2	6.4	0.9	2.5	3.6	1.8	4.0	0.8
Mature Tigers	**7.2**	**7.1**	**4.6**	**16.3**	**4.6**	**8.2**	**13.3**	**5.9**	**9.6**	**4.6**
E. Asia exc. China	**8.7**	**8.4**	**5.1**	**17.6**	**8.0**	**12.1**	**20.0**	**7.7**	**13.6**	**8.9**
Bangladesh	0.1	0.0	0.0	0.3	0.1	0.1	0.0	0.0	0.5	0.0
India	0.5	0.1	0.1	1.2	0.8	0.6	0.2	0.2	1.6	1.0
Pakistan	0.1	0.0	0.0	0.6	0.0	0.2	0.0	0.0	0.8	0.1
Sri Lanka	0.0	0.0	0.0	0.1	0.1	0.1	0.0	0.0	0.3	0.1
S. Asia	**0.7**	**0.1**	**0.2**	**2.2**	**1.0**	**1.0**	**0.2**	**0.3**	**3.2**	**1.2**
Argentina	0.3	0.1	0.1	0.3	0.7	0.3	0.1	0.3	0.3	0.8
Brazil	1.4	0.4	1.0	1.6	2.5	0.9	0.3	0.9	0.7	2.1
Mexico	0.6	0.9	0.7	0.5	0.6	2.4	2.9	2.7	2.5	0.9
L. America	**2.3**	**1.3**	**1.8**	**2.3**	**3.8**	**3.7**	**3.3**	**3.9**	**3.4**	**3.8**
Sub-Saharan Africa	**0.6**	**0.2**	**0.2**	**0.5**	**1.4**	**0.4**	**0.1**	**0.3**	**0.5**	**1.1**

Notes: See Table 4.3.
Source: Calculated from UN Comtrade database.

9–10 per cent, assuming that world markets continue to grow at past rates.

It is useful in this context to look at the structural dynamism of exports across East Asian countries. The correlation values for exports in 1990 and 1997 are shown in Figure 4.2 – the higher the coefficient, the more stable the structure and the lower the coefficient the more changeable the structure. MHT exports are shown separately from total manufactured exports, and the world export structure is shown as a reference point. The world export structure, not surprisingly, is extremely stable, with MHT products showing a slightly lower degree of stability. The most stable country in the region is Hong Kong SAR, China, which goes together with its weak recent export performance. The most

Figure 4.2   Correlation between export structures, 1990–97

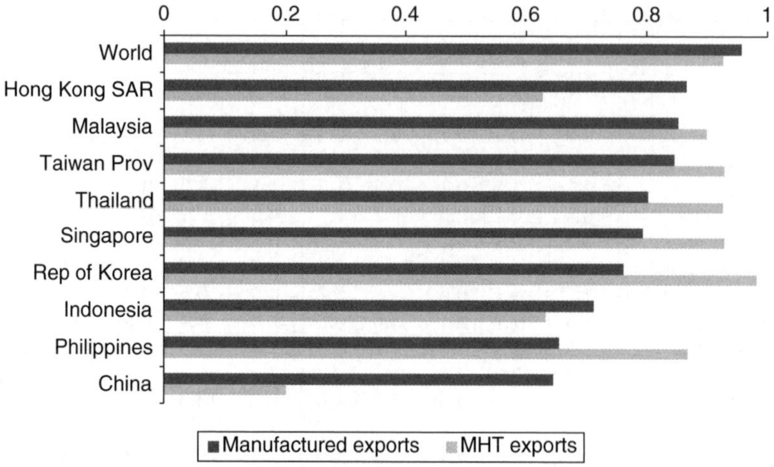

Note: Figures are for Pearson correlation values for exports by each country in 1990 and 1997. The lower the value, the more dynamic the export structure duing the period. There are 180 items in manufactured exports and 75 in MHT (SITC 3 digit, rev. 2).

dynamic country is China. Many high-tech exporters in the region exhibit surprising stability in their MHT export structures: the same product groups that dominate their exports in 1990 continue to do so in 1997.[9] By contrast, China shows a large change in the structure of its MHT exports – there are a large number of very dynamic new products in this period. These figures imply a massive competitive threat from China to exports by the region and elsewhere, not just in the expected low-technology categories but also in high-technology ones. Note, however, that China's ability to sustain this threat entails significant structural upgrading of its industrial sector, particularly as increases in market share after a certain threshold are bound to become more difficult. We return to these issues later in the analysis of capabilities.

Manufactured export performance at the product level

The above section treated manufactured exports at a fairly aggregate level. We now analyze export performance at the three-digit SITC level for China and selected comparators for 1990–97. Given the large number of products, we have to be selective. We focus on the fastest growing products within the electronics (the main HT products of

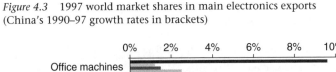

Figure 4.3 1997 world market shares in main electronics exports (China's 1990–97 growth rates in brackets)

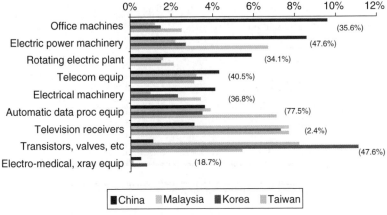

Source: Calculated from UN Comtrade database.

interest to the region), MT and LT categories, with different comparators in each.

Figure 4.3 starts with the nine most dynamic electronics and electrical products in world trade, comparing China with Malaysia, the Republic of Korea and Taiwan Province of China. It also shows the rate of growth of Chinese exports in the period. Some results are surprising. China now has the largest market share of the group in several high-tech products, including office machines and telecommunications equipment. It is also advancing rapidly in automatic data processing equipment and is dominant in sophisticated electrical equipment. On the other hand, it has relatively low shares in TV receivers and semiconductors. This can, however, change if these industries gear up for exports, exploiting scale and agglomeration economies in the gigantic domestic market, and leading TNCs start to use it as a regional or global sourcing base.[10]

Let us now take a selection of dynamic MT products. We take as comparators large exporters like Republic of Korea, Mexico and Brazil (the new Tigers, with relatively weak capital goods industries, are not important here). We include products in which China is not a major exporter, like passenger vehicles and engines and motors. Figure 4.4 shows world market shares and Chinese export growth rates.

China dominates in exports of three items, with its products accounting for nearly 20 per cent of the world radio receiver and

Figure 4.4   1997 world market shares in dynamic MT products (China's 1990–97 growth rates in brackets)

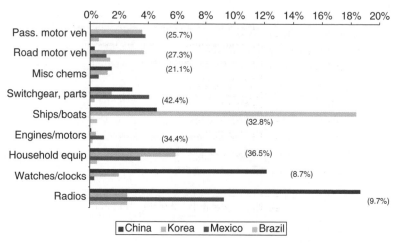

Source: UN, Comtrade SITC 3-digit level rev. 2.

12 per cent of watch and clock exports. China is practically absent in the global automotive value chain, though it has a large and growing domestic auto industry. As with the TV industry, it is conceivable that it will become a major exporter if it gears itself up for an assault on export markets, taking advantage of domestic scale economies and supplier base.

Finally, we look at the most dynamic LT exports (Figure 4.5). The comparators here are India, Indonesia and Thailand. China expectedly dominates each of the products, with world market shares of over 15 per cent in five product categories, led by toys and sporting goods and followed by footwear. It also exhibits very high recent growth rates in almost all its main LT exports.

These competitiveness patterns reinforce the previous argument. The Chinese threat is much broader based than LT (where it is indeed very large). Moreover, even where it is not yet apparent it is possible that China will emerge as a major competitor in products with a large domestic base – and that it will do so with the speed that marks its entry elsewhere. Since China is not obliged to depend heavily on TNCs, as are many other dynamic exporters in the developing world, it can also launch an autonomous challenge along Korean or Taiwanese lines.

Figure 4.5 1997 market shares for dynamic LT products
(Chinese 1990–97 growth rates in brackets)

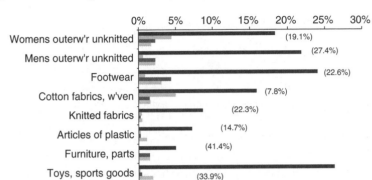

Source: Calculated from UN Comtrade SITC 3-digit level rev. 2.

Comparing competitive capabilities

We now consider some structural drivers of competitiveness (UNIDO, 2002): human capital, technological effort, inward FDI, technology imports and infrastructure. This list does not include all relevant factors, but it covers the quantifiable ones. As noted at the start, the measures are not perfect but they are useful as proxies – and they provide relevant information.

Human capital

Two aspects of human capital and competitiveness are considered here: *wage costs* and *skills*. Comparable data on manufacturing wages are not available for each comparator, and Figure 4.6 shows the ratio of wages in selected countries for manufacturing as a whole (Figure 4.6a) and for some low and high technology activities (Figure 4.6b).

China's wage advantage is immediately obvious. For manufacturing as a whole, wages in the Philippines are nearly five times higher (and Philippines is cheaper than Malaysia or Thailand). Those in the Republic of Korea are nearly 25 times, and in Taiwan Province of China nearly 20 times higher. The labour cost reasons for relocating production to China are clearly strong, and will become compelling where other productive inputs and business costs are comparable.[11]

Figure 4.6a   Ratio of wages to Chinese wages in all manufacturing

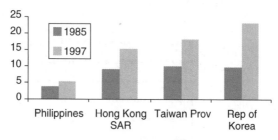

Source: ILO, Labour Statistics Database; Bank of Korea and Taiwan Monthly Bulletin of Statistics.

Figure 4.6b   Wage ratio in selected low and high-tech activities

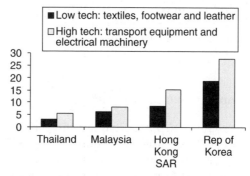

Source: ILO, Labour Statistics Database and Bank of Korea.

What is perhaps more important is that China's wage advantage is significantly higher in high-tech than low-technology activities. If all else were equal – and this is a big 'if' in high technology activities, where supporting clusters, advanced skills and sophisticated institutional support is vital – the pressure to move to China will be even greater. Needless to say, this threat is particularly keen for advanced countries in the region, but it will also affect less developed countries that are seeking to attract relocating activities. China will compete not just on low wages, of course, but also on the size and capabilities of its industrial sector and institutions. These are also formidable.

As far as skills are concerned, we rely on formal enrolment data. This is not an ideal measure of the skill base for industrial activity. It does not take into account the quality, completion and relevance of formal education and it ignores other forms of skill formation (on-the-job learning and formal training provided by employers). However, it is the only available measure and does capture the base of education on which other skills are grafted.

China has a good primary education system with universal enrolment, and a strong secondary education with over two-thirds of the relevant age group enrolled. This is lower than the mature Tigers (particularly Republic of Korea and Taiwan Province of China) and Argentina, but higher than the other Asian countries (particularly South Asia), Mexico, Brazil and Sub-Saharan Africa (the lowest in the developing world). Its strong base of literacy and numeracy gives China a vital competitive edge, particularly in activities needing basic worker and technical skills. However, it remains relatively weak in modern management skills. According to Wu (1995), this is the biggest obstacle today to promoting and diffusing new technologies at the firm level. By contrast, technical personnel in China are reputedly of high quality; Stavis and Gang (1988) find that Japanese and US managers praise Chinese engineers and technicians for their commitment and creativity.

However, the present level of technical skills may not be sufficient to sustain China's future competitiveness as the industrial sector adopts advanced modern technologies, and as technologies themselves become more skill-intensive. We can compare its creation of high-level technical manpower (as measured by tertiary level enrolments in science, mathematics and engineering) with that of other countries (Table 4.6).

China has the highest absolute number of tertiary technical enrolments in the developing world, accounting for over 18 per cent of the total (this is the third highest in the world, after the US and Russia). India used to be higher than China in 1985, but has declined since then (and now ranks fourth in the world). In terms of the *intensity* of skill creation (as a percentage of the population), however, China ranks relatively low, below other Southeast Asian countries, India and Latin America (but higher than other South Asian countries and Sub-Saharan Africa). This suggests that China has a structural skill weakness: this may not show up at this time but is likely to affect its competitive position in the longer term. As long as the gap remains, the more advanced countries in the region should be able to keep ahead of Chinese competition in skill and technology-intensive exports.

These figures are, of course, very rough proxies for skill creation, and the impact of relatively low enrolments is likely to be very unevenly spread in manufacturing industry. It is not possible to gauge which

Table 4.6 Tertiary technical enrolments

	1985			1997		
	Total enrolment ('000)	% of pop	Developing country share	Total enrolment ('000)	% of pop	Developing country share
China	**821.5**	**0.08**	**17.1**	**1 221.0**	**0.10**	**18.3**
Thailand	81.8	0.16	1.7	110.5	0.19	1.7
Malaysia	13.8	0.08	0.3	26.7	0.13	0.4
Indonesia	137.3	0.08	2.9	439.1	0.23	6.6
Philippines	271.5	0.47	5.6	387.3	0.55	5.8
New Tigers	**504.4**	**0.18**	**10.5**	**963.6**	**0.27**	**14.4**
Hong Kong SAR	27.5	0.49	0.6	30.2	0.49	0.5
Korea Rep.	320.7	1.65	6.7	742.5	1.65	11.1
Singapore	18.1	0.71	0.4	14.1	0.47	0.2
Taiwan Prov.	115.7	0.59	2.4	226.8	1.06	3.4
Mature Tigers	**482.0**	**0.72**	**10.0**	**1 013.6**	**1.31**	**15.2**
E. Asia	**986.4**	**0.28**	**20.5**	**1 977.2**	**0.46**	**29.6**
Bangladesh	97.9	0.09	2.0	90	0.08	1.3
India	1,233.8	0.15	25.6	1,086.3	0.12	16.3
Pakistan	28.5	0.03	0.6	63.4	0.05	1.0
Sri Lanka	13.8	0.08	0.3	15.4	0.08	0.2
S. Asia	**1 374.0**	**0.14**	**28.5**	**1 255.1**	**0.10**	**18.8**
Argentina	210.9	0.68	4.4	162.3	0.47	2.4
Brazil	225.9	0.16	4.7	289.3	0.18	4.3
Mexico	375.7	0.48	7.8	400.1	0.44	6.0
L. America	**812.5**	**0.34**	**16.9**	**851.7**	**0.29**	**12.8**
SSA(1)	58	0.02	1.2	185	0.05	2.7

Source: UNESCO, Statistical Yearbook (various).
Note: (1) Sub-Saharan Africa excludes South Africa for 1985, but not for 1997.

activities will be most affected. Large-scale industry is likely to be able to recruit sufficient skilled manpower, and urban areas are likely to do better than rural ones. It is the small and medium-sized enterprises outside major urban centres that are likely to suffer most from growing skill constraints.

In the neighbouring region, the competitive threat from China in terms of skills is likely to affect the new Tigers (with the exception of Philippines) the most. While they have higher enrolment rates, China is expanding its higher education system more rapidly and has 'elite' universities to spearhead its technological upgrading (World Bank, 2000). It has the advantage of a huge body of technical manpower, with concomitant advantages of critical mass, externalities and agglomeration benefits. These may allow it to overtake many neighbours in skill-based activities and the medium technology end of activities currently dominated by the mature Tigers. Needless to say, it will also challenge Latin America in the same way that it challenges the new Tigers. South Asia and Sub-Saharan Africa in general will not have a skill advantage over China.

This does not mean that competing countries will not have skill advantages in specific industrial activities – after all, industrial countries compete intensely with each other with roughly similar human capital bases. What it does mean is that the Chinese threat will not be confined to the low end of manufacturing, but will spread to the entire range. Competitors will have to find particular activities, processes and products in which they specialize in this competitive spectrum.

Technological effort

Technological effort takes many forms and occurs in most facets of manufacturing activity. As such, it is nearly impossible to quantify at the enterprise or industrial, not to speak of national, level. The only technological measure available is formal R&D. While this captures the 'tip of the iceberg' of technological activity, it is relevant as an indicator of technological effort in newly industrializing countries. For these countries, absorbing complex new technologies does need R&D, and R&D assumes growing significance for competitiveness as they need to build upon imported technologies to bring better products to the market. We use R&D financed by productive enterprise as the relevant indicator rather than total national R&D, which includes many elements not relevant to industry.

Figure 4.7 shows 1998 enterprise-financed R&D for China and all the comparators deflated by MVA. It immediately highlights a major com-

Figure 4.7   R&D spending/US$1000 of total and MHT MVA (1998)

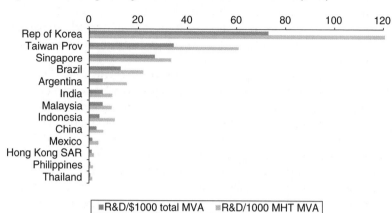

Source: Calculated from UNESCO, *Statistical Yearbook* (various); UNIDO, WIDR 2002.

petitive weakness in Chinese industry: it invests little in formal technological effort in relation to leading developing competitors. This has
clearly not held back its export dynamism so far, since much of it has
been based on imported technology and specialization in low-level
functions.

However, as industrial development continues and wages rise this
will have to change. Chinese enterprises will have to invest more in
formal R&D to absorb complex technologies and build upon them to
establish their own competitive edge. Foreign affiliates engaged in
complex activities will also have to raise their R&D investments (as
they are doing in Singapore and, to a much lesser extent, in Malaysia).

The innovative capability of Chinese industry can also be assessed by
its 'output', the most readily measurable of which is patenting. The
best way to compare this across countries is to take patenting in an
international location rather than at home. Most studies use patents
taken out in the US. These show that China ranks relatively low. For
instance, the total accumulated patents by 1998 came to 721 for
China, compared to 11 293 for Republic of Korea, 16 286 for Taiwan
Province of China, 1174 for Hong Kong SAR, China, 603 for Singapore
and 659 for India.[12] The figures for Latin America are 1074 for Brazil,
1756 for Mexico and 806 for Argentina. In terms of total spending on
enterprise funded R&D, of course, China performs better. It is larger
than all other newly industrialized economies (NIEs) apart from
Republic of Korea and Taiwan Province of China (Figure 4.8). While

Figure 4.8 Total R&D financed by productive enterprises in 1998 (US$ million)

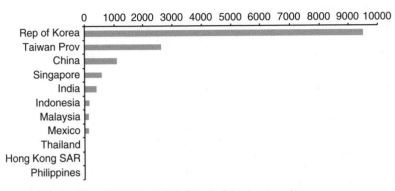

Source: Calculated from UNESCO, *Statistical Yearbook* (various issues).

total R&D is not a good indicator of the *intensity* of technological effort, it does suggest that China has an R&D base that achieves minimum critical mass in a range of industrial activities. Moreover, it is backed by massive government R&D in defence and basic science (the government accounts for about 50 per cent of total national R&D), which is likely to have strong spillover benefits. It should also be noted that Chinese enterprises spend more on R&D, despite the legacy of planning and government ownership, than many formerly socialist economies in Central and Eastern Europe (where government institutions conducted R&D on behalf of enterprises). In China there appears to be considerable technological autonomy in the enterprise sector; WTO accession will probably boost their effort.

Despite these strengths (and proven technical competence in many non-industrial fields), China faces technological weaknesses in competing with the mature Tigers and industrialized countries (World Bank, 2000). This will constrain its ability to compete in genuinely high-technology segments of manufacturing for some time to come. However, it will pose a serious threat to countries lower in the technology scale, including the new Tigers, India and Latin America.

Inward FDI

China is now the leading developing country recipient of FDI, vying with the US for first place in the world as a whole. However, the Chinese government has till now had a strong preference for joint ventures rather than foreign-controlled affiliates, to enhance the transfer of managerial and technical know-how to local enterprises (Tsang, 1995). Joint ventures accounted for half of the number of projects involving foreign investment in 1998 (*Chinese Statistical Yearbook 1999*), the majority being for original equipment manufacture production.

Figure 4.9 shows the values of inward FDI and China's share in inward FDI in East Asia and the developing world. Foreign investors have, as noted, been major drivers of China's export success, and can be expected to continue being so for the foreseeable future. The composition of FDI inflows is changing. In the initial stages, most export-oriented FDI came from neighbouring Tiger economies, particularly from (and through) Hong Kong SAR, China; some of these inflows included 'round-tripping' by Chinese firms. Over time, advanced industrial countries have accounted for larger shares of FDI, mostly to serve the domestic market (Graham and Wada, 2001). However, many of the traditional TNCs are also turning to export activities and, given the competitive advantages of producing in China, are likely to raise their export role.

However, for China to be fully integrated into the international production systems of large TNCs may call for a more transparent and liberal economic environment than has existed till now. WTO entry, if followed by policy changes on FDI, local content, corporate governance and so on, will certainly lead to a better investment climate and so strengthen TNC-based competitive advantages. It should therefore

Figure 4.9   Inward FDI flows (US$ million)

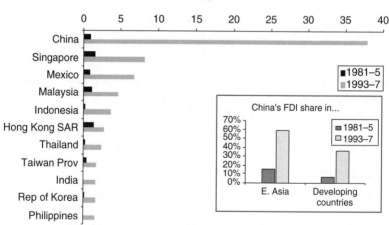

Source: World Bank, WIDR 2001: UNCTAD, *World Investment Report* (various issues).

lead to greater incorporation into dynamic integrated production systems in high-tech activities.

The bulk of foreign export-oriented activities in China is in the SEZs and is not strongly linked to the domestic economy. Much of it has consisted of the simple assembly of LT products. As the data show, however, there has been considerable upgrading of the skill and technology content of FDI related exports (though the UN export data do not distinguish exporters by origin). This is also confirmed by case studies of Taiwanese investors cited in Graham and Wada (2001). It is hardly surprising that this should be so, since this is the pattern for export-oriented FDI in many other Southeast Asian countries. The countries that have, however, extracted the maximum gains from TNCs in terms of local linkages, technological upgrading and the launching of R&D have been those with a clear and efficient industrial policy. The prime example in the region is Singapore, but there are others, like Ireland in Europe. There is no reason why China should not do something similar. It has technological ambitions and a penchant for industrial policy – what remains to be seen is whether it is able to design and implement appropriate policies post-WTO. The Singaporean and Irish strategies worked only because of strong skill creation, where China is at a disadvantage, and a clear private-sector orientation.

If skill and policy handicaps are overcome, however, China will mount a major competitive challenge to its neighbours in attracting export-oriented FDI and using it to upgrade and diversify its exports. Many high-tech TNCs are setting up large facilities in China, some presumably in preference to other locations in the region. If the domestic industrial sector undergoes restructuring quickly – at least in areas of export interest to TNCs – the attractions of China as a major sourcing base will increase enormously. We may then expect to see a surge of exports not just by foreign affiliates but also by subcontracting and OEM arrangements with local firms.

Importing foreign technology in other forms

China does not have large payments of royalties and technical fees abroad in relation to the size of the economy (Figure 4.10). Its payments in 1998 were smaller than most other comparators apart from India and the Philippines. Note that these payments capture the import of advanced technology both by foreign affiliates and by local firms, so that licensing is not really an alternative to FDI. In fact, the highest per capita royalty payments in the world (by Ireland and

Figure 4.10 Technology licence payments abroad (US$ million)

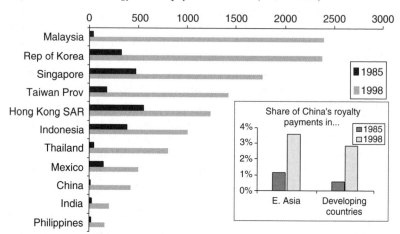

Source: UNIDO (2002).

Singapore) are from countries with a dominant TNC presence (UNIDO, 2002). The low figures for China suggest thus that it is lagging in accessing the newest, most valuable technologies from overseas.

This has clearly not been a constraint on export competitiveness in the early stages. However, as it moves into more sophisticated technologies for the export market its licensing costs are bound to rise (TNCs may have been willing to provide advanced technologies more cheaply to China for domestic market operations, but will not for export activities). WTO rules will probably require China to liberalize on controls on technology licensing in any case, so that we can expect to see payments grow rapidly in the future. As it stands, however, inadequate technology access may be restraining China's competitive challenge to the region.

ICT infrastructure

Infrastructure in general is a major factor in competitive advantage, and that for ICTs is of growing importance in technology-intensive activities. China lags behind many comparators in the region by available measures of ICT (Figure 4.11); Latin American countries (only Mexico is shown in the figure) are also ahead of China. However,

Figure 4.11 Main ICT indicators (1998)

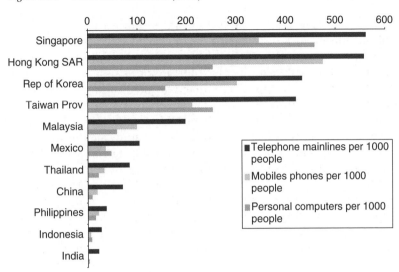

Source: World Bank, WIDR (2001).

China does better in terms of telephones per 1000 people than Philippines, Indonesia and India.

The modernization of the ICT sector in China is at the top of its political and economic agenda. The government is making a major effort to extend the telecommunication networks and develop a fibre optic network linking eastern provinces with high population densities (Mansell and Wehn, 1998). In addition, the Ministry of Post and Telecommunications is launching links to other countries in the region.

Most of this infrastructure is concentrated in major urban and industrial areas (Mansell and Wehn, 1998). While this may be undesirable for equity reasons, it will strengthen the competitive position of manufacturing exporters. However, China has a long way to go before it catches up with the leaders in the region. Its competitive threat is thus likely to be concentrated on the second tier of countries. South Asia is again likely to face direct and intense competition in areas where ICT infrastructure is an important factor. Sub-Saharan Africa is below South Asian levels, and so will be even more threatened (if, that is, it had to compete in ICT intensive industries).

Conclusions

The picture this analysis gives of China's competitive challenge is mixed. Some indicators suggest a major challenge across the board, in products and countries. Others suggest a narrower challenge, focused on the low to medium level of technology and skills and on countries like the new Tigers and South Asia (and, by implication, in Africa and Latin America). However, such inferences are extremely difficult to draw from the kind of data used here. Only specific industry and firm level analysis for each location can show the nature and dimensions of the emerging competitive scene – there are many determinants of competitiveness that can only be meaningfully analyzed at this level.

Moreover, the past is not necessarily a good guide to the future in this dynamic setting, with large policy changes, rapid technical progress and shifting location strategies on the part of TNCs. We noted at several points that China was rapidly building up its capabilities, and that some import-substituting industries may become export-oriented as incentive structures change. At the same time, other governments, acutely conscious of the Chinese competitive threat, are also enhancing their competitive capabilities.

More important, even if China were to bring its competitive capabilities nearer to the level of the Tiger economies, the threat would only be for industries that were unable to upgrade or specialize, and to countries that could not support upgrading adequately. As in the developed world, trade would become more and more within industrial sectors than across them: intra-industry trade would allow plenty of 'room for everyone'. *The real competitive challenges is thus for countries to develop the base of capabilities, skills and infrastructure that would allow them to specialize efficiently in activities that allow for continued income growth.*

This being said, there will be short- to medium-term stresses for countries as they adjust to the new giant entrant into many activities in which they have established export markets. The most direct stresses in the region will be felt by the new Tigers, but mature Tigers like the Republic of Korea and Taiwan Province of China will also face increasing pressures to upgrade more rapidly. If they fail to respond adequately, they will suffer from lower competitiveness. China may not be content to attract lower levels of technology from them but may seek to challenge them directly in the most complex activities and functions. There is practically no activity in which China cannot build up a competitive edge; the evidence suggests that it is already doing so with amazing rapidity.

For countries specialized in low-technology exports and without the ability to upgrade capabilities rapidly – South Asia and Africa are good examples – the challenge will be much more serious and longer term, at least in the manufacturing sector. They will face enormous threats in their main areas of (current or future) export interest, without the ability to move into more complex products ahead of their rival. There may be some potential for intra-industry specialization and trade but in many low-technology products this potential is fairly limited.

To conclude, therefore, China *will* be a major competitive threat to many developing countries as liberalization proceeds and it gains access to world markets. The threat will be most immediate and intense in labour-intensive products and processes, but it is broader and is likely to quickly affect the entire technological spectrum. How broad and rapid it is will depend, however, on China's ability to improve its competitive capabilities – and here it lags in many critical respects behind most countries in the region. The Chinese government seems to be very aware of these deficiencies and, if recent performance is any guide, its improvement will be quite fast. WTO accession, if properly handled, can accelerate the process. This is not to say that its internal restructuring will not pose serious challenges – it will, but any reasonable forecast would lead policy-makers elsewhere to take its threat very seriously indeed.

Notes

1 The net impact of China's WTO entry on primary product exports by other developing countries is likely to be positive, as it opens its markets and industries to resources and raw materials from abroad (see Chapter 3).

2 For a broader application of the analytical approach presented here see *World Industrial Development Report 2002*, forthcoming (UNIDO, 2002).

3 According to the 1999 *Statistical Yearbook* of the Government of China, 52 per cent of Chinese manufactured exports come from local firms and the remainder from 'foreign invested' firms. See the official website at http://www.stats.gov.cn/english/yearbookml.html.

4 Hong Kong SAR, China remains the largest foreign investor in China. Its share in China's overall FDI has, however, decreased from 60 per cent in the early 1990s to around 47 per cent in 1998. US investment in China accounted for almost 9 per cent for 1998, higher than that of Japan (data from source cited in previous note).

5 Note, however, that logistical, political and strategic considerations may lead TNCs to keep spread export-oriented facilities over different countries even if one country (China) were cheaper in absolute terms.

6 The first step is to separate *primary products* from *manufactures*. We use a classification that places primary products with even a slight degree of processing into the manufactures category (Lall, 2001, Chapter 4). We then classify manufactured products into four groups by technology. This classification draws upon but amends and adapts standard classifications used by the Organization for Economic Cooperation and Development (OECD) and the US National Science Foundation.

1. *Resource-based manufactures* (RB): mainly processed foods and tobacco, simple wood products, refined petroleum products, dyes, leather (not leather products), precious stones and organic chemicals. RB products can be simple and labour-intensive (for example, simple food or leather processing) or capital, scale and skill-intensive (for example, petroleum refining or modern processed foods). Competitive advantage in these products arises generally – but not always – from the local availability of natural resources.

2. *Low-technology manufactures* (LT): such as textiles, garments, footwear, other leather products, toys, simple metal and plastic products, furniture and glassware. These products tend to have stable, well-diffused technologies largely embodied in capital equipment, with low R&D expenditures and skill requirements, and low economies of scale. Labour costs tend to be a major element of cost and the products tend to be undifferentiated, at least in the mass-produced (non-fashion) end of the scale. Barriers to entry are relatively low; competitive advantages in products of interest to developing countries come from price rather than quality or brand names.

3. *Medium-technology manufactures* (MT): these are 'heavy industry' products like automobiles, industrial chemicals, machinery and relatively standard electrical and electronic products. MT products tend to have complex but not fast-changing technologies, with moderate levels of R&D expenditure but advanced engineering and design skills and large scales of production. In engineering products, there is emphasis on product design and development capabilities as well as extensive supplier and subcontractor networks. Barriers to entry tend to be high, not only because of capital requirements, but also because of strong 'learning' effects in operation, design and, in certain products, product differentiation. Innovation in the engineering segment increasingly involves cooperation in the value chain, between manufacturers, suppliers and sometimes customers (in large items of equipment).

4. *High-technology manufactures* (HT): complex electrical and electronic (including telecommunication) products, aerospace, precision instruments, fine chemicals and pharmaceuticals. The products with advanced and fast-changing technologies and the complex skill needs have the highest entry barriers. The most innovative ones call for large R&D investment, advanced technology infrastructures and close interactions between firms, universities and research institutions. However, many activities, particularly in electronics, have final processes with simple technologies, where low wages can be an

important competitive factor. The high value to weight ratio of these products allows segments of the value chain to be broken up and located across long distances.

There is a steady progression up the technology ladder from resource-based to high-technology activities (though there can be exceptions of the type noted above). The last two categories, medium and high technology, can be taken to comprise the 'complex' end of industrial technology, while the first two, resource-based and low technology, comprise the 'simple' end.

7 South Asia has, with the exception of India, a simpler industrial structure than China. Over time, the most growth has been in labour-intensive activities, at the expense of resource-based activities. In part this reflects the relative lag in industrial development in most South Asian countries; in part it also reflects the rapid growth of labour-intensive exports from the region (below). India is an interesting contrast to China: with a similar heavy industry base, it has been less successful in complex exports. Its manufactured exports are still overwhelmingly in low-technology and resource-based products. The marked mismatch between the Indian export and MVA structures suggests low competitiveness in its complex industries as well as the inability to attract TNCs into export-oriented activities (Lall, 2001). Note that Sub-Saharan Africa's MHT share lies between South Asia and Latin America, though with a higher weight of resource-based activities than both. This reflects the dominance of South Africa in the region (South Africa has a strong base in medium-technology activities like steel, chemicals and mining equipment). Without South Africa, African industry is much more dominated by resource-based activities (53 per cent); MHT only accounts for 24 per cent of MVA, the lowest of any region.

8 In some cases (for example, Pakistan, Sri Lanka, Indonesia) this simply reflects the small starting base of HT products; in others it shows the dynamism of HT exports in general and the insertion into integrated production systems. A regression analysis of export growth and structure for 87 industrial and developing countries for 1985–98 confirms that the technological structure of exports does matter for export growth. Specialization in complex exports promotes growth, particularly for more industrialized countries (UNIDO, 2002).

9 Philippines has recently emerged as a strong HT exporter by virtue of the growth of semiconductor products, but its export structure for MHT products remains fairly unchanged. See Lall (2001) for an analysis of its recent export performance *vis-à-vis* other new Tigers.

10 For example, this is already happening in the TV industry. The Republic of Korea's LG Electronics is to invest US$1 billion to produce flat-screen TV displays, with an annual capacity of 30 000 units, and manufacturing liquid crystal displays with an annual capacity of 250 000 units (business news of the 18 July 2001, chinaonline.com). Hitachi is setting up a liquid crystal display plant (75 000 units per month), primarily to meet local demand, but may well extend into exports in the future if it proves competitive.

11 Another cost incentive for the relocating to China is the cheapness of industrial land. For instance, monthly rentals for factory space in the

Shenzen SEZ were about US$2–4 per square metre compared to about US$40 in Hong Kong SAR, China (Boulton, 1997).

12　Data are from NSF (2000).

References and bibliography

Boulton, W. R. (1997), 'Electronics manufacturing in the Pacific rim', World Technology Evaluation Center panel report, Loyola College, Maryland.

Dicken, P. (1998), *Global Shift: Transforming the World Economy* (London: Paul Chapman Publishing Company), third edition.

Doner, R. and Brimble, P. (1998), 'Thailand's hard disk drive industry', Emory University (USA) and The Brooker Group (Thailand), draft.

Graham, E. M. and Wada, E. (2001), 'Foreign direct investment in China: effects on growth and economic performance', in P. Drysdale (ed.), *Achieving High Growth: Experience of Transitional Economies in East Asia* (Oxford: Oxford University Press).

Lall, S. (2001), *Competitiveness, Technology and Skills* (Cheltenham: Edward Elgar).

Mansell, R. and Wehn, U. (1998), *Knowledge Societies: Information Technology for Sustainable Development* (Oxford: Oxford University Press).

NSF (2000), *Science and Engineering Indicators 2000*, Washington DC: National Science Foundation.

Stavis, B. and Gang, Y. (1988), 'Babcock and Wilcox Beijing Company Ltd', *China Business Review*, July–August, 10–12.

Tsang, E. W. K. (1995), 'The implementation of technology transfer in Sino-foreign joint ventures', *International Journal of Technology Management*, 10 (7/8), 757–66.

UNIDO (2002), *World Industrial Development Report 2002* (Vienna: UNIDO), forthcoming.

World Bank (2000), 'China's development strategy: the knowledge and innovation perspective', draft, 16 August 2000.

Wu, C. (1995), 'Great leap or long march: some policy issues of development of the internet in China', *Telecommunications Policy*, 20 (9), 699–711.

Zhang, Z. (2000), 'Accession of China to the World Trade Organization: Impact on the manufacturing sector in China', UNIDO: paper presented to the Asia-Pacific Regional Forum on Industrial Development (Shanghai).

5

Industrial Environmental Management and the WTO Rules: the Case of China

Ralph A. Luken and Casper van der Tak

F13   Q51
F14   Q56
P33   P23

Introduction

China's accession to the World Trade Organization (WTO) is expected to increase the industrial environmental challenges that the country already faces and will require enhanced and even new policy measures if China wants to minimize potentially adverse effects.

Accession would yield the following results:

1. Changes in the scale, sectoral composition and technology of the industrial sector would affect both positively and negatively the pollutant potential of industry.
2. Expansion of international trade in products and services, primarily in textiles and apparel; however, these are increasingly subject to new trade barriers based on standards or various forms of certification.
3. Widening and deepening international capital inflows, which would facilitate the utilization of foreign technology, with the potential to be either environmentally friendly or unfriendly.
4. Increased openness of the Chinese economy, which would facilitate acquiring knowledge of environmentally sound technologies (ESTs) developed abroad even without involving foreign direct investment (FDI).
5. Increased international competition might motivate additional calls for less stringent environmental regulations. These calls would aim at reducing environmental compliance costs with the objective of enhancing the competitiveness of the Chinese manufacturing

industry. Additional pressure to weaken environmental regulation is all the more likely to emerge, especially from the industrial sector and the governmental unit responsible for industrial development, since WTO accession will negatively affect the capital-intensive sectors in which the ailing state-owned enterprises (SOEs) are dominant. However, abatement costs in China (and elsewhere) are very low in relation to total production costs, so that environmental leniency – a potential result of this pressure – would only result in a marginal improvement in competitiveness. Ensuring that environmental standards can be achieved in the most cost-efficient way and reducing the regulatory burden would have a stronger effect on industrial competitiveness than easing environmental standards – while avoiding adverse environmental consequences.

The magnitude of the challenges outlined above warrants careful analysis by those parties in China concerned with industrial environmental management. In addition, they call for ensuring that effective environmental policies exist and that, whenever necessary, new ones are put in place to respond to such challenges.

Three challenges

Base case projections and simulation design

Accession by China to WTO includes a complex package of trade and investment liberalization. Based on the China–United States market accession agreement, this chapter quantifies the impact of the following four aspects: (i) tariff reductions on industrial products; (ii) elimination of quotas on industrial products by 2005; (iii) agricultural trade liberalization, that is, tariff reduction for agricultural products and introduction of tariff rate quota (TRQ) system for agricultural goods; and (iv) phasing out of the Multi-Fibre Arrangement (MFA) quota on textiles and clothing under the WTO Agreement on Textiles and Clothing (ATC). China's textiles and apparel exports to the North American and European Union (EU) markets will be subjected to accelerated MFA quota growth by 2004 similar to that applying to other developing countries, and the remaining export quota restrictions will be terminated in the year 2005. Therefore, the analysis at best captures only one part of the expected change. It does not take into account other major aspects of WTO membership, such as reduction of barriers in service trade and foreign investment, protection of intellectual property rights, securing market access, enforcement of commitments, and cooperation in dispute settlement.

The consequences of WTO accession have been analyzed with a Computable General Equilibrium (CGE) model, which simulates the behaviour of different actors in the economy, assuming simple objectives for these actors such as profit-making enterprises and welfare-maximizing consumers (Zhai and Li, 1998). This type of model is especially suitable for short- and medium-term simulations. The simulation assumptions and scenario design are described briefly in Annex I, and the results of the simulation are presented below.[1]

Changes in industrial production-scale

Broadly speaking, industrial pollution emissions in any country depend upon three characteristics (Chua, 1999): (i) the scale of industrial production – given that pollutant emissions are a non-product output of manufacturing activities; (ii) the sectoral composition of industrial production – given that some sectors are more resource-and-energy intensive than other sectors; and (iii) the technique or method of industrial production in any given sector – given that it is possible to produce goods with different technology combinations. The CGE modelling effort describes changes in two of the characteristics: scale and sectoral composition. It does not capture productivity growth as it is based on fixed technological coefficients.[2] In addition, the CGE modelling effort generates information on regional effects, which suggest that the advanced coastal provinces would benefit the most from accession in terms of investment, GNP growth, employment generation etc. and that interior provinces would hardly benefit, if at all.

The main efficiency and macroeconomic indicators under the four scenarios of China's WTO accession are given in Table 5.1. The results are presented as deviations from the base case in the year 2010, with and without WTO accession. The results show that China will benefit from its WTO accession in terms of real gross domestic product (GDP) and social welfare. In 2010, China's real GDP will increase 1.1 per cent compared with the base case (E1). Private consumption would increase 1.05 per cent, indicating the benefits to consumers from the trade liberalization.

Many factors determine these general equilibrium results. Generally, the large gains in GDP result from an enhanced efficiency of resource allocation through increased specialization according to comparative advantage and through more intense competition, necessitating greater efficiency. But two other factors also contribute to GDP growth:

Table 5.1   Major macroeconomic variables under China's WTO accession scenarios in the year 2010 (percentage change relative to the base case)

	Whole WTO accession package (E5)	Tariff and non-tariff barrier reduction on industrial products (E2)	Agricultural trade liberalization (E3)	MFA elimination (E4)
GDP	1.10	0.15	0.42	0.27
Consumption	1.05	0.19	0.47	0.21
Investment	0.81	−0.05	0.44	0.15
Exports	17.13	4.26	1.99	6.51
Imports	16.75	4.16	1.98	6.36
Government revenue	0.96	−1.62	−0.10	1.88
Urban households income	1.47	0.14	0.96	0.18
Rural households income	0.71	0.26	0.03	0.24
Terms of trade	−1.07	−0.31	−0.12	−0.45
Real exchange rate	0.14	1.73	0.88	−1.79

Source: Zhai and Li (2000).
Note: The results of E5 do not equal to the sum of E2, E3 and E4 due to the interactive effects

(i) removal of high protection rates would induce higher real deprecia-tion rates, thus enhancing the international competitiveness of China's industries; and (ii) elimination of MFA would further increase the competitiveness of China's textiles and apparel, leading to export expansion for those sectors.

Changes in industrial production – sectoral composition

While the aggregate results of the WTO accession scenarios show the overall welfare gains resulting from lower price distortions and expanded trade, they reveal only part of the story. Economy-wide efficiency gains are not distributed uniformly across sectors. Thus, it is necessary to investigate the adjustment in sectoral output and trade that would be induced by China's accession to the WTO. For the pur-poses of this paper, only the impact on the manufacturing sector is shown (see Table 5.2).[3]

The elimination of the MFA quota would significantly enhance China's export competitiveness in textiles and clothing. Exports of tex-tiles and apparel would increase by 100 per cent and 114 per cent respectively. The production of textiles and apparel would increase by 23.4 per cent and 38.6 per cent respectively. There are other notable

Table 5.2 Estimated changes in manufacturing output and trade by year 2010 further to China's WTO accession

	Output		Imports		Exports	
	Billion Yuan	%	Billion Yuan	%	Billion Yuan	%
More polluting sectors						
Paper and printing	-3.8	-0.4	6.1	5.5	-0.6	-4.0
Chemicals	-23.6	-1.2	33.6	8.9	-2.9	-1.8
Chemical fibres	29.2	9.9	42.9	74.0	0.6	2.6
Building materials	1.1	0.0	0.8	2.5	-1.8	-2.3
Petroleum refining	-38.0	-4.3	40.1	62.7	-2.7	-3.3
Primary iron and steel	-31.9	-2.0	5.0	3.2	-1.7	-3.0
Non-ferrous metals	-10.4	-1.7	-0.6	-0.6	-1.2	-3.8
Somewhat polluting sectors						
Processed food	14.0	1.1	1.0	2.9	4.8	5.4
Beverages	1.7	0.3	3.5	49.1	0.1	1.0
Tobacco	-0.1	0.0	2.5	29.2	0.0	-0.2
Textiles	491.7	23.4	183.7	96.2	325.3	100.4
Leather	-8.0	-1.7	0.2	0.4	-8.3	-6.7
Metal products	-15.5	-1.2	5.1	4.7	-5.1	-3.9
Electric machinery	-29.8	-1.8	9.5	6.0	-14.2	-6.1
Electronics	-58.1	-4.0	9.7	2.2	-24.9	-5.7
Automobiles	-165.2	-17.3	82.5	375.4	-2.0	-12.3
Other. transport equipment	-3.6	-0.5	3.4	3.1	-2.8	-4.8
Less polluting sectors						
Sawmills and furniture	1.5	0.2	2.0	5.7	-1.8	-3.2
Apparel	378.9	38.6	12.9	64.1	359.5	114.3
Rubber and plastics	-20.7	-1.8	3.4	5.0	-7.5	-4.6
Metal products	-15.5	-1.2	5.1	4.7	-5.1	-3.9

Table 5.2 Estimated changes in manufacturing output and trade by year 2010 further to China's WTO accession (*continued*)

	Output		Imports		Exports	
	Billion Yuan	*%*	*Billion Yuan*	*%*	*Billion Yuan*	*%*
Machinery	−34.8	−2.5	14.1	6.6	−4.2	−5.2
Instruments	−13.7	−6.3	5.7	6.0	−7.2	−8.3
Special equipment	−13.9	−1.6	19.0	5.9	−1.8	−4.3
Other manufacturing	−8.9	−1.9	1.7	12.0	−7.3	−12.0
Unclassified						
Social articles	−12.3	−2.1	1.8	5.0	−13.9	−6.9
Medicine	0.5	0.1	1.2	13.0	−0.1	−0.4

Source: Zhai and Li (2000).

changes in sectoral composition. Some food sectors would also increase their output and exports, as they would benefit from a reduction in the cost of imported agricultural intermediate input. However, those sectors with high protection, such as the automobile industry, petroleum refining and beverages, would experience a sharp increase in imports. The lower import prices would induce consumers to substitute imports for domestic products, resulting in a dramatic decline in output. All capital-intensive sectors, even those that are not highly protected, such as electric machinery, electronics and instruments, would experience fairly large contractions of production because of the higher capital cost. The rapid expansion of labour-intensive sectors, especially textiles and apparel, would attract capital away from other manufacturing industries, and the large amount of labour released from previously highly protected agricultural sectors would jointly push up the rental price of capital relative to labour.

Since capital-intensive industries are normally also the more polluting ones, this suggests that the change in sectoral composition as a result of WTO accession might reduce total pollutant discharge into the environment. It is possible to test this hypothesis in a roundabout way, using data from the World Bank Industrial Pollution Projection System (IPPS) on pollution intensities (see Table 5.3). The IPPS data for 1995 can be combined with the information in Table 5.2 on the sectoral impact of WTO accession to get a rough estimate of the impact of accession on total pollutant loads of some key pollutants. Note that these estimates are not indisputable; 1995 intensity coefficients are used, and the subsectoral matching between the World Bank and China is not perfect. Hence the results presented should be regarded as tentative. Nevertheless, it is possible to get an idea of the impact of WTO accession on total pollution loads.

For most pollutants considered herein, WTO accession would result in an increase in total pollutant load, although in some cases this is lowered by WTO accession (see Table 5.4). The factor driving the increase in pollutant load would be the increase in GDP (approximately 1.1 per cent increase after WTO accession, as shown in Table 5.1). The isolated effect of sectoral change on pollutant loads induced by WTO accession is shown in the last column. As can be seen, the sectoral composition effect of WTO accession in all cases lowers the total pollutant load. These results indicate that WTO accession would have some beneficial effect on sectoral composition, shifting production away from polluting to less polluting industrial sectors. In a real sense, it contributes to a reduction of the pollution intensity of the Chinese economy.

Table 5.3 Pollution intensities; kg per 1000 RMB (1995)

Sector	ISIC	COD	TSS	SO$_2$	Smoke	Dust
More polluting sectors						
Paper	3 411	68.913	31.872	6.970	4.720	0.618
Chemical	3 511	3.018	5.006	5.001	2.729	0.770
Chemical fabric	3 513	3.365	1.942	2.299	1.311	0.170
Petroleum	3 530	0.452	0.254	1.931	0.855	0.199
Building and other non-metal products	3 699	0.351	1.119	10.564	6.488	39.622
Ferrous metal products	3 710	1.034	8.195	4.560	2.213	5.468
Non-ferrous	3 720	0.240	1.524	7.887	1.843	1.471
Somewhat polluting sectors						
Food, beverages and tobacco	3 110	7.742	3.496	1.987	1.468	0.115
Textile	3 210	1.058	0.413	1.505	0.823	0.025
Leather	3 230	2.527	1.045	0.727	0.461	0.033
Printing	3 420	0.181	0.210	0.628	0.317	0.001
Pharmaceutical products	3 522	3.456	0.835	1.685	0.970	0.015
Metal products	3 810	0.104	0.142	1.004	0.641	0.065
Less polluting sectors						
Coking	3 540	3.194	1.273	9.249	7.432	7.958
Rubber	3 559	0.322	0.285	1.737	0.806	0.144
Plastics	3 560	0.095	0.088	0.775	0.308	0.006
Machinery	3 820	0.116	0.099	0.507	0.374	0.066
Other products	3 900	0.904	1.122	1.208	0.820	0.374

Source: Hettige et al. (1995) 'The industrial pollution projection system', Policy Research Working Paper 1431, World Bank.

Table 5.4   Impact of WTO accession on total pollution loads

	WTO accession, total impact, scale effect	WTO effect on sectoral composition
COD	0.34	−0.76
Total suspended solids	−0.35	−1.45
SO$_2$	0.65	−0.45
Smoke	0.80	−0.30
Dust	−0.31	−1.41

Note: Compiled from data contained in Table 5.2 and in Table 5.3

However, the real growth of the Chinese economy causes a net increase in pollutant loads (at least for some pollutants).

Note that the estimate of changes in pollutant loads does not take into account the Chinese environmental protection policies that are in place. China has a fairly well developed environmental protection system, and protection of the environment has been a major Chinese policy in recent decades. Quite favourable results have been achieved.

China aims to further reinforce its environmental protection policy. For example, the tenth Five-Year Plan (FYP), which was passed in March 2001, contains specific targets for the percentage of forest cover and green cover in completed urban areas by 2005. More to the point, the tenth FYP contains a target of a 10 per cent reduction in total pollutant load, and a reduction of total sulphur dioxide (SO$_2$) emissions in acid rain control areas by 20 per cent, both also to be achieved by 2005. Seen against the background of the vast economic growth in China (a GDP growth rate of 7 per cent is assumed), these targets imply a considerable reduction in pollution intensity of production.

Assuming that China will aim to achieve these targets, the above results imply that the sectoral composition effect of WTO accession will help China to reduce its pollution intensity. However, this aspect is negated by the increased growth rate. Overall, WTO accession means that China will need to achieve an even greater reduction in pollution intensity, which increases the importance for China to select pollution-control strategies that lower the regulatory burden imposed on industry.

Changes in export patterns

A notable outcome of China joining the WTO would be a significant expansion of foreign trade. The increase of exports and imports by two is the effect of compounded accelerating growth. The difference in annual growth rate of exports between accession case and base case is 1.6 percentage points. The processing trade (high import content in exports) accounts for more than half of China's total trade. Therefore, growth of exports will result in a corresponding growth of imports, increasing the pressure on real depreciation rates and contributing to further growth of exports. This factor has partly contributed to the rapid increase of China's trade dependence in the last 20 years and explains the significant effect on trade expansion that China's WTO accession would have.

The removal of tariff and non-tariff barriers (NTBs) is only one factor that would contribute to a significant surge in imports after China joins the WTO. The export growth due to further realization of China's comparative advantage in labour-intensive products would also contribute to an increase of imports. The expansion of labour-intensive production drives up the demand for capital and technology-intensive equipment, on the one hand, and increases the demand for semi-processed products and intermediate input on the other hand. As was pointed out earlier, there is a large proportion of processing exports in China's total exports (exports and imports would increase 17.1 per cent and 16.8 per cent respectively). China's trade expansion would be significant when it becomes a member of the WTO. This structural feature in China's foreign trade sector makes export growth particularly important as a factor explaining China's import growth. Its effects are shown clearly in the sharp increase of imports of textiles, apparel and chemical fibres because processing imports account for more than 90 per cent of total imports in these industries.

Acceleration of FDI

Accession to the WTO would most likely accelerate the already rapid growth in gross capital formation, particularly that based on FDI. During the period from 1980–99, gross fixed capital formation increased from US$71.0 billion to US$368.4 billion. FDI started accounting for a significant share of gross capital formation only in the 1990s, when it increased from 2.8 per cent in 1990, peaked at 15.1 per cent in 1994 and declined to a still respectable 10.5 per cent in 1999 (World Bank, 2001a). As can be seen in Table 5.1, investment is expected to increase over the baseline by 0.81 per cent as a result of accession to the WTO. This suggests that the rapid growth will continue and, with the easing of investment restrictions due to WTO accession, that the share of FDI will increase, probably exceeding its peak in the 1990s.

The economic rationale for reducing pollution intensity

Environmental pollution is and will continue to be a serious matter in China (PRCEE, 2001). Regarding air pollution, progress was made during the 1990s due to the government closing down some heavily polluting enterprises and to reductions in production levels. However, industry remains the dominant source of SO_2 and soot (same as Total Suspended Particulates), and ambient air quality for these two pollutants exceeds ambient air quality standards in most major cities. Regarding water pollution, significant progress was made during the 1990s with the rate of discharge of industrial wastewater (in millions of tons) meeting the national standards increasing from 50 to 67 per cent. However, many water bodies remain severely degraded, partially due to the discharge of industrial pollution. The amount of industrial solid waste generation increased as did the accumulated storage during the 1990s.

As described in the previous section, China will need to achieve an even greater reduction in pollution intensity to maintain its gains to date in reducing total industrial pollutant discharges. In order to do so, the State Environmental Protection Administration needs to reassure the industrial sector and its representatives in government bureaux that the benefits to society from reducing negative health and welfare effects would exceed the costs to industry of reducing industrial pollution. Such decisions, or at least the economic rationale for them, need to take into account, first, the extent to which the benefits of the effort would exceed the costs, and secondly, the extent to which the effort would or would not have a significant economic impact (price increases, employment loss and plant closing) on the competitive position of Chinese industry, which will already face increased cost competition as a result of trade liberalization.[4]

Unfortunately, there are only limited data and analyses about the Chinese situation to address the benefit-cost or economic impact concerns about intensification of industrial environmental regulation. Consequently, this section will briefly summarize experiences of other countries that have had to address the same issues as well as including the available data about China. The data, however, are not sufficient because they do not permit one to determine whether the marginal benefits of pollutant reduction are equal to or greater than the marginal costs, nor do they permit one to take into the full economic impact on specific industrial sectors.

Environmental benefits and costs

Several benefit-cost assessments, including those for specific pollutants, have been undertaken with regard to environmental programs in the US (Anderson and Kobrin, 2000). A comprehensive review of the aggregate annual benefits of all environmental regulations showed them to be US$162 billion (in 1996) with total annual costs of US$144 billion (Office of Management and Budget, 1997). A more comprehensive assessment, limited to air pollution regulations, found that the annual costs of compliance were US$523 billion and that the annual benefits ranged from US$5.6 trillion to US$49.4 trillion (USEPA, 1997).

Unfortunately, there are few pollutant- or sector-specific estimates of the benefits and costs of environmental regulations for any developing country similar to those for the US. At best there are some rough estimates for some countries and some urban areas. Here a few national and urban damage assessments from all sources of pollution as a percentage of GDP or gross national product (GNP) are listed. (None of these assessments takes into account global environmental damage due to ozone depletion or global warming.) The data in most of the studies are not sufficiently disaggregated to assign a share of damages to the industrial sector. Summary estimates are presented in Table 5.5. It can be seen that environmental damages with only partial coverage of pollution sources and limited monetization of benefits are a significant percentage of GDP or GNP.

No empirical estimates of the national costs for pollution control as a percentage of GDP, similar to those for the US and several EU countries, are available for developing countries. The best estimate that can be arrived at for developing countries is to assume that their expenditure on pollution control, in the long run, would be similar to that of developed countries (OECD, 1996). The percentage of GDP spent for environmental compliance is, on average, 1.6 in developed countries. Of that, one-quarter is spent on industrial environmental compliance and three-quarters on municipal, transport and other sectors.

Comparing environmental damage as a percentage of GDP in various developing countries to an expenditure of 1.6 per cent of GDP suggests that, in aggregate, the social benefits from reducing environmental damage would exceed the sum of private and public costs of that reduction. In all cases cited, the estimated damages as a percentage of GDP exceed the costs of pollution reduction as a percentage of GDP. In the case of China, the potential environmental gains appear to be very high compared with the costs, both in terms of average and marginal benefits and costs. In addition to those rough estimates, more rigorous

Table 5.5 Estimates of environmental damage and assumed costs of abatement

Country/city	Pollutants/sources and effects	Estimated damages as percentage of GDP/GNP	Assumed abatement costs as percentage of GDP
Brazil	Only health care costs associated with water and air pollution	2.0 of the GDP	1.6
China	Mainly industrial sources	4.0 of the GNP[a]	1.6[b]
India	Only health impact of water and air pollution	3.3 of the GDP	1.6
Jakarta (Indonesia)	Health impact of air and water pollution	3.5 of the GDP of Jakarta	1.6
Mexico	Estimates of environmental damage costs	2.5 of the GDP	1.6
Thailand	Health effects from air pollutants	1.2–5.0 of the GDP	1.6

[a] The estimate prepared by the World Bank, which uses a more appropriate valuation procedure, is 8 per cent of GNP (World Bank, 1998).
[b] The actual number for China is probably lower. The estimate for the current period is 0.8 per cent and the target for the tenth FYP is 1.2 per cent of GDP.

Sources: Brazil: Seroa and Fernandez (1996); China: Guang (1997); India: Brandon and Homman (1995); Indonesia: World Bank (1994); Mexico: Margulis (1996); Thailand: O'Connor (1996).

estimates of the benefits and costs of pollution in Asia are slowly appearing – such as the one prepared by a team of Chinese researchers working with the World Bank, who estimated the relationship between air pollution and mortality from respiratory disease in Beijing. Their analysis showed that removal of 100 tons of sulphur dioxide from Beijing's atmosphere could save one statistical life, which is defined as the probability of one person dying when one million people are exposed to a risk of one in a million (see Annex II). Abating one ton of SO_2, controlling only 10 per cent of the emissions, would cost a large plant approximately US$3 per year. Thus the costs of abating 100 tons would cost approximately US$300. A value of at least US$1 000 000 per statistical life saved (the minimum value used by the US Environmental Protection Agency (USEPA)) would imply a benefit-cost ratio of 3000 to 1. Even taking the much lower estimate of the value per statistical life (US$8000) that has been proposed for China would still yield a benefit-cost ratio of 24 to 1 (Dasgupta et al., 1997).

Magnitude of compliance costs

According to the OECD, the costs of environmental compliance for developed countries is believed to be in the range of 1–5 per cent of production costs (OECD, 1997a).[5] The word 'believed' is used deliberately because, as discussed by Nordström and Vaughan (1999), only the US has systematically collected data on the costs of pollution abatement. The average cost for all industrial subsectors was 0.6 per cent of the value of shipments and between 1.5 and 2 per cent for the more pollutant-intensive subsectors (see Table 5.6). Those percentages are relatively modest compared with the other outlays for production inputs.[6]

Such a modest outlay should not be allowed to mask the difficulties that were encountered by resource-and-energy-intensive industries in the investment phase of complying with environmental regulations. As pointed out by Low (1992), using a more detailed breakdown of the same data from the US Census Bureau, the costs of pollution abatement were as high as 3.2 per cent of the value of shipments. Nor should it mask the fact that some categories of small firms in developed countries, particularly in urban areas, could not comply with the regulations and were forced to close or to consolidate.

It should be noted that the percentage of pollution control costs for industry are on the high side in developed countries, in particular the US, because they have relied on the uniform application of performance standards and the use of end-of-pipe technology to achieve

Table 5.6 Pollution abatement operating costs by industry in the US (1993)

SIC[a]	Industry	Pollution abatement operating costs (US$ millions)	Value of shipment (US$ millions)	Abatement cost/ value of shipment (percentage)
29	Petroleum and coal products	2 793	144 715	1.93
28	Chemicals and allied products	4 802	314 744	1.53
33	Primary metal industries	2 144	142 384	1.51
26	Paper and allied products	1 948	133 486	1.46
32	Stone, clay and glass products	544	65 574	0.83
31	Leather and leather products	52	9 991	0.52
34	Fabricated metal products	742	175 137	0.42
22	Textile mills products	280	73 951	0.38
30	Rubber and miscellaneous products	409	122 776	0.33
20	Food and kindred products	1 368	423 257	0.32
37	Transportation equipment	1 327	414 614	0.32
36	Electronic and other electric equipment	716	233 342	0.31
24	Lumber and wood products	279	94 547	0.30
25	Furniture and fixtures	137	47 349	0.29
38	Instruments and related products	383	136 916	0.28
39	Miscellaneous manufacturing industries	85	42 426	0.20
35	Industry machinery equipment	488	277 957	0.18
27	Printing and publishing	266	172 737	0.15
21	Tobacco products	33	28 384	0.12
Total		18 796	3 054 287	0.62 (average)

Note: Pollution abatement operating costs include capital depreciation of the abatement equipment; filters and another material, salaries and wages for operational personnel.
[a] SIC: Standard industrial classification.
Source: US Census Bureau as cited in Nordström and Vaughan (1999).

environmental norms. With hindsight, achieving ambient standards aimed at protecting human health and welfare and a more judicious mix of prevention and abatement measures would have resulted in a lower level of expenditure.

In recent years reasonably comparable data at the subsector level are available for China. All industries are required to submit an environmental statistics report annually to the provincial Environmental Protection Bureau (EPB). The data allow an estimate to be made of abatement costs (depreciated capital costs and operation and maintenance costs) for air and water pollution control; there are no data for solid waste disposal. Estimates of annualized abatement costs for the year 1999 are given in Table 5.7. Although there is some variation in the reported percentages over the past few years, it can reasonably be concluded that pollutant abatement expenditures are reasonable with an average of 0.4 per cent of gross industrial output values and for the more pollutant-intensive industrial categories in the range of 1.0 to 1.5 per cent.

Several case studies undertaken in developing countries suggest that the costs would be the same or even less: between 1 and 3 per cent. UNIDO summarized many of those case studies to arrive at such an estimate of the cost of environmental compliance by industry as a percentage of production costs (UNIDO, 1995).[7] A few of the findings from the UNIDO review should be highlighted. In the Philippines, pollution abatement costs as a percentage of total costs were less than 1 per cent for the sectors studied. The only sectors where those costs exceeded 2 per cent were in the agriculture and energy sectors (UNCTAD, 1995). In Argentina, two large pulp and paper companies were not significantly affected by a pollution control investment of 8 per cent of its capital stock, whereas a smaller firm in the same area was forced to close as a result of environmental regulations. Also in Argentina, only a few of the 35 firms in the leather sector experienced difficulty in complying with environmental norms, and two that attempted to comply declared bankruptcy (Chudnovsky, Lugones and Chidiak, 1995).

In summary, there is some economic evidence, drawn from the experience of other countries as well as from China, that the government of China ought to continue to pursue, as it had proposed in the tenth FYP, an aggressive effort to reduce industrial pollution in spite of the increased competitiveness pressures that industry will experience as a result of WTO accession for two reasons.[8]

First, it appears that the social benefits of environmental improvement would exceed the private costs of compliance given the

Table 3.7   Pollution abatement operating costs by industry in China in 1999[a]

ISIC No.	Industrial sector	Total abatement costs for liquid and gaseous emissions (RMB 1000 Yuan)	Gross industrial output values (RMB 1000 Yuan)	Abatement costs/gross industrial output values (percentage)
3411	Paper and allied products	1 161 900	89 232 500	1.30
3720	Smelting and pressing of non-ferrous metals	907 800	126 416 000	0.72
3511	Chemicals and allied products	2 654 100	379 227 600	0.70
3710	Smelting and pressing of ferrous metals	2 101 900	307 687 900	0.68
	Mining and quarrying	1 720 400	262 632 100	0.66
	Electricity, gas and water supply	1 713 900	265 559 500	0.65
3530	Petroleum refining and coke products	1 602 100	260 547 100	0.61
	Chemical fibre products	376 900	68 365 100	0.55
3513	Non-metal mineral products	1 157 100	210 700 100	0.55
3720	Textile industry	900 200	272 448 300	0.33
3210	Metal products	251 700	92 028 000	0.27
3810	Pharmaceutical products	270 000	99 171 600	0.27
3522	Other industries	353 600	160 871 100	0.22
	Leather and fur products	115 500	53 515 300	0.22
3230	Food, tobacco and beverage products	800 600	480 213 600	0.17
3110	Rubber products	60 100	45 974 400	0.13
	Machinery and electronic products	985 900	919 114 300	0.11
3559	Plastic products	28 700	3 326 300	0.09
3820	Printing and publishing industry	11 900	19 578 200	0.06
3560				
3420				
Total		17 174 400	4 146 608 900	0.41

[a] This estimate is based on data for one year. Data are available for five years and an average over the five-year period would be more representative and probably result in a rank ordering of sectors based on percentage spent on pollution control similar to the rank ordering for the US (Annex II). Also, it is not clear to the authors of this paper the extent to which the reporting plants are in compliance with environmental standards.

Source: Center for Environmentally Sound Technology Transfer (CESTT) based on the China Environment Yearbook 2000, China Environment Yearbook Publishing House.

significant existing and projected increase in pollutant discharges by industry. Second, there appears to be sufficient evidence that the costs of compliance with environmental regulations by industry in China would be within a reasonable 1–3 per cent of production costs and should not affect the competitive position of most enterprises. However, this claim should not mask the problems that will be encountered by resource-and-energy-intensive sectors in mobilizing the funds for the large capital investments that will be required to comply with environmental norms nor the general financial difficulties that will be encountered by existing small plants in complying with environmental norms.[9] The difficulties will clearly be severe for some small firms that do not have access to technological information, space for locating pollution control equipment or capital at a reasonable rate of interest.

Policy options

Current situation

China's current industrial environmental management regime applies in varying degrees to all four basic categories of environmental regulation utilized in OECD countries (OECD, 1997b). These are command and control, economic incentives, voluntary arrangements and information disclosure (PRCEE, 2001).

First, the regime applies directly to enterprises a command and control approach (licensing) to regulate behaviour affecting the environment. The State Environmental Protection Administration (SEPA) has formulated concentration-based national guidelines, 29 for the most common water pollutants and 13 for the most common air pollutants. Its licences stipulate that pollution-control treatment should take place within specified time limits. It has required preparation of Environmental Impact Assessments (EIAs) since the early 1980s and through the three Synchronization Programmes, it reviews the design of pollution-control equipment, supervises the construction of treatment plants and monitors operation of the newly constructed plants. The primary limitation to this approach is that these laws and regulation have not been adequately enforced for a variety of reasons.

Secondly, it applies economic instruments to modify behaviour, using financial incentives and disincentives such as charges, taxes and fines, to improve environmental performance. EPBs apply a pollution levy system (PLS) that imposes a fee on pollutant concentrations exceeding the standards. This fee depends on the difference between actual concentrations and the standards. The EPBs also levy tariffs on wastewater treatment and solid waste disposal and in some cases apply environmental taxes, which apply to all emissions/effluents, even those inside the pollutant concentration limits. The primary limitations to this approach are that the levy is applied to only one pollutant (the one on which the assessed penalty is the highest; in other words, the one that exceeds the standard most, if weighted by the charge rate) and the charge rate of the levy system is too low, resulting in only a small effect on enterprise performance.

Thirdly, SEPA has promoted three voluntary instruments that aim to co-opt participation of firms into improving environmental performance. These instruments are environmental labelling (started in 1991), cleaner production (first large-scale demonstration project in 1993 and formulation of Cleaner Production Law in 2000) and environmental certification procedures (introduced in 1997). The primary limitation with these voluntary instruments is their limited application within the country. The total number of enterprises that have conducted cleaner production audits since 1993 is still less than 500 and, as of February 2001, approximately the same number of enterprises and institutions have obtained ISO 14001 certificates (Shi, 2001).

Fourthly, there are no information disclosure programmes comparable to those in developed and developing countries that aim to use public pressure to improve environmental performance. There does exist, however, a formal procedure for citizen complaint within EPBs and there are ongoing experiments with the use of information disclosure approaches in Zhenjiang and Hohhot cities.

Responding to changing patterns of industrial production

Clearly, there are several possibilities for improving the performance of China's industrial environmental management programme. In each of the four categories summarized above, numerous large and small changes are needed to improve the efficiency and effectiveness of the individual instruments.[10]

We propose that SEPA consider formulating an industrial environmental management strategy that aims to reduce in the most cost-effective manner the greater environmental risk that would result from increased pollutant intensity.

First, SEPA should go from testing a public disclosure programme, which is similar to the World Bank Programme for Pollution Control Evaluation and Rating (PROPER) for Indonesia, and implement a national programme. A programme similar to PROPER for China would not require significant resources to design and implement and has the prospect of being as successful as the one in Indonesia. In the pilot phase of PROPER, the project involved 187 enterprises, of which 115 were classified as red (somewhat polluting) and 6 were classified as black (very polluting). After only one year of operation (1996), the number of plants classified as black declined from six to three and the number of plants classified as red declined from 115 to 108 (World Bank, 1999).

Secondly, EPBs should encourage factories when renewing their environmental licences to undertake a cleaner production assessment. These assessments in most instances highlight significant areas of the waste of materials, water and energy, and result in companies taking corrective measures to reduce wastage. Experiences in China have resulted in plants investing in prevention measures that would reduce their cost for complying with environmental norms. For example, a major manufacturer of fine chemicals in China, specializing in the production of additives for the processing of higher polymer materials, implemented cleaner production measures that reduced water use by 80 per cent and chemical oxygen demand by 95 per cent; and capital investment needed for pollution control equipment by 25 per cent, the annualized costs of its operation by 15 per cent and increased output by 25 per cent (Berkel, 1996). Many other demonstrations in China have showed similar potential for cleaner production to lower the costs of compliance as well as the costs of production undertaken by the China National Cleaner Production Centre in such diverse sectors as cement, distillery and fertilizer. In most cases, however, financially attractive process change was not sufficient to reduce pollutant discharge to the extent necessary to comply with the environmental standards. Pollution-control measures, which would have a negative cost impact, would be necessary for compliance.

Thirdly, SEPA should assist provincial and city EPBs to target major sources of pollutant discharge for compliance with environmental norms. In many situations, only a few sources account for most of the pollutant discharge and those sources, usually being larger plants, have lower per unit costs of pollution reduction than smaller plants. For example, an area-wide environmental management plan for Dong Nai Province, Vietnam, estimated that controlling water pollution at three out of 55 plants would reduce the organic pollutant load discharged by 90 per cent (UNDP/UNIDO, 1998). A more compelling example comes from the experience of Brazilian regulatory agencies, which rank factories according to size and risk, and target the largest or most risk-creating factories almost exclusively. In the case of Rio de Janeiro, the regulatory agency ranked several thousand factories based on their pollution discharge, and on health and welfare risks. After this ranking, they found that targeting only 50 large factories in the highest risk category could reduce 60 per cent of the state's serious industrial pollution. In addition, they found that targeting 150 plants in the medium-risk category could reduce an additional 20 per cent of the serious pollution and that by targeting 300 plants out of several thousand in the smallest-risk category, an additional 10 per cent could be reduced (World Bank, 1999).

Fourthly, SEPA should monitor and support the provincial EPBs to ensure that they actually bring the targeted factories, that is, those in the high-risk category, into compliance with environmental norms in order to maintain the credibility of the national effort to protect the environment. The EPBs need to advise the enterprises on how to formulate an integrated pollution prevention-and-control strategy, provide technical advice and access to funding sources for both process and pollution control technologies, formulate a transparent and publicly available compliance schedule, monitor compliance with environmental norms and take effective enforcement action. If the action of the EPBs does not result in compliance by the targeted enterprises, then SEPA should bring its weight to bear on them and their respective industrial associations formed under the State Economic and Trade Commission to comply with environmental norms.

Reducing potential barriers to exports

As described above, China's exports in certain sectors would expand with accession to the WTO. The most notable sectors would be textiles and apparel. Even within other sectors, such as the manufacture of electronics and household appliances, some enterprises would significantly expand their exports and have the potential to become multinationals. For example, Haier, the largest manufacturer of white goods in China, recently built an assembly plant in the US (*China Daily*, 19 December 1999).

Many of the firms that would benefit from the export opportunities would do so as suppliers in global value chains. These buyer-driven chains are dominated by a few transnational corporations (TNCs) or retailers that design and market, but do not manufacture the product. These TNCs and retailers impose many demands on their suppliers in terms of quality, quick response and frequent deliveries. These demands, often based on standards or the need for various forms of certification, need to be addressed by Chinese exporters or they will become new entry barriers. In the early 1990s, these demands included calls for improved environmental performance and more recently they have called for improvements in social, in addition to environmental, performance because of concerns raised by developed country consumers and international non-governmental organizations (NGOs).

Expanded capacity for environmental management systems (EMS) (ISO 14000)

SEPA introduced ISO 14000 certification procedures in 1997. After an initial testing period, SEPA established a Registration Board for Environmental Auditors and several environmental management and consulting centres were established to conduct ISO 14000 certification. However, the uptake of ISO 14000 is slow for several reasons. First, most firms, except for large state- and foreign-owned enterprises, are not aware of the advantages of introducing an environmental management system. Second, the certification centres cannot meet the current demand, both for certification and provision of professional advice on how to set up an environmental management system. Third, firms in the more established sectors, such as metallurgy and building materials, cannot meet the environmental norms required to be certified by the government programme.

Increasing environmentally sound technology (EST) content in FDI

The availability and cost of cleaner technologies and pollution-control equipment will fall with the increasing openness of national economies such as will result from accession to WTO.[11] Research by the World Bank examined the uptake of cleaner technologies in steel (continuous casting and electric arc furnaces) and pulp and paper (thermo-mechanical pulping) production in 50 countries. The research indicated that open economies led closed economies in the adoption of cleaner technologies by a wide margin (World Bank, 1999). Similarly, a more recent study of the uptake of the electric arc furnace in 30 steel-producing countries over 25 years also found that the technology is diffused faster in countries with more open trade-policy regimes (Reppelin-Hill, 1999). In finer as in broader analysis, there are some examples of how the openness of the economy can have a beneficial effect on the availability and costs of cleaner technology. One such example is the response of the tannery sector in India to a ban by Germany on the import of leather goods preserved by pentachlorophenol (PCP) and coloured with dyes containing formalde-hyde and benzidine (Wiemann et al., 1994). The initial problems of the leather industry occurred mainly due to a lack of testing facilities to determine PCP content and a lack of PCP substitutes. Those problems took a few months to resolve until testing centres were set up and the tanneries in India obtained information on where to purchase substitutes. In order to facilitate the import of substitutes, such as 2-thiocyanatomethylbenzothiazole (TCMTB) and para-chloro-meta-cresol (PCMC), the government of India reduced the import duty from 150 to 50 per cent *advalorem*. In contrast, the leather industry in Argentina did not face the same initial problems as a result of the PCP ban because its liberal trade policies had already made those chemicals more accessible (Chudnovsky, Lugones and Chidiak, 1995).

The potentially increased content of FDI in gross capital formation presents an opportunity for China to incorporate the latest developments in EST into FDI. Often, the larger investors already understand the advantages of incorporating such developments in their investment projects as these advances reduce operating costs (by reducing energy, water and raw materials related costs) and reduce the volume of waste that needs treatment by pollution-control equipment. However, not all foreign investors take the same approach and procedures are needed to ensure that the potential of EST is considered in all investment projects.

Studies outside China have found that enforced environmental laws influence corporate behaviour. For example, there are several indicators of investments in EST as a consequence of enforcement of environmental legislation in Mexico (Ruijters, 1995). Consequently, all the measures suggested above for improving the enforcement of environmental legislation, including increasing the pollution levy, would be useful not only for reducing pollutant discharge, but also for influencing corporate behaviour in regard to decisions about EST.

China can already take advantage of existing institutional arrangements to promote the use of EST in investment decisions. First, it could widen the scope of the EIA process. Currently, EIAs are mainly used to identify pollution control measures to mitigate the adverse consequences of proposed industrial projects and not to influence either process technology choice or location decisions. The process could be modified to require reporting on resource utilization requirements of the proposed and alternative-process technologies and justifying why the most efficient ones in terms of water, raw materials and energy use are not deployed. Secondly, China could strengthen its technological infrastructure (primarily research and development institutions) to set up demonstrations to upgrade and improve the environmental performance of technologies that are currently being deployed in China. Unfortunately, the funding for such institutions that already have too many objectives is limited and the funding achieves limited results because of the lack of industry input into the research efforts (Alam, 2001).

This opportunity to accelerate the update of EST in FDI should not be missed not only because of its immediate impact on the efficiency of foreign firms within China, but also because of the indirect productivity gains through the 'contagion' effect (Démurger, 2000). The non-competitive and non-exclusive nature of EST hardware and software found in foreign firm investments can generate externalities, which can be transmitted by the training of workforces and links between domestic and foreign firms.

Conclusions

China would confront three significant industrial environmental challenges as a result of its WTO accession. First, in spite of the positive environmental effects of the change in the sectoral composition of the manufacturing sector, the overall increase in the production of manufactured goods will most likely increase the pollution intensity of industry. Secondly, accession would result in an expansion of international trade in products and services, primarily in textiles and apparel, which are increasingly subject to new trade barriers based on standards or the need for various forms of certification. Thirdly, accession would widen and deepen international capital flows, which could increase the utilization of foreign technology that has the potential to be either environmentally friendly or unfriendly.

Although based on limited empirical evidence from China, there is sufficient economic justification for China to push ahead with a demanding industrial environmental strategy in spite of the increased cost competition that industry will experience in the light of trade liberalization. First, it appears that the social benefits of environmental improvement would exceed the private costs of compliance given the significant existing and project pollutant discharges by industry. Secondly, there appears to be sufficient evidence that the costs of compliance with environmental regulation with environmental standards by industry in China would be within a reasonable range of 1–3 per cent of production costs and should not affect the competitive position of most enterprises.

In the light of the environmental challenges generated by WTO accession and compelling economic reasons, China needs to continue and perhaps accelerate its efforts to reduce pollutants from industry as well as other sources. Several reviews have suggested how this might be done. In addition, China might consider a targeted strategy for addressing industrial pollution. The strategy would go beyond its current efforts in that it would seek the most cost-effective pollutant reductions in situations that currently and in the future will pose the greatest environmental risk.

Annex I

Since China's WTO accession schedule will be phased in over a transition period of 5–8 years, a recursive dynamic model was utilized to assess the impact of China's WTO membership. Basically, this means that optimal economic decisions are made over a short to medium time horizon, and that these decisions take place at different times. The dynamic model captures the changes of industrial structure, factor composition and comparative advantage of China in the next ten years.

The base-case projection for the next ten years (one point in time, the year 2010) is established first. This determines a reference growth trajectory, in the absence of trade or other reforms. It assumes that China will continue its grain self-sufficiency policy, and import quota of agricultural goods will grow at 3 per cent annually from 2000–10. Four scenarios are considered in reference to the baseline scenario of 2010. The first scenario focuses on the tariff reduction and the elimination of quotas on industrial products that China has offered for the WTO accession. The sectoral reduction rates of import tariff are aggregated, based on the Harmonized Commodity Description and Coding System tariff schedules for the period of 2000–8 in the China–US agreement and weighted by 1997 ordinary trade data. In this scenario, the growth rate of the import quota for petroleum refining and automobiles will also be accelerated in 2000–5 and the quantitative restriction will be eliminated in 2005. The second scenario focuses on the agricultural trade liberalization. The TRQ system will be introduced to replace the current quota system for rice, wheat, corn, cotton, wool, vegetable oil and sugar. Moreover, the tariff for other agricultural goods will also be reduced. The third scenario focuses on the impact of MFA elimination. In this case, China faces accelerated quota growth rate for its textiles and clothing exports, and the quantitative restriction will be terminated in 2005. The last scenario combines all three aspects of

Table 5.8   Summary of simulation design assumptions

Experiment	Description
E1	*Base case*
	– real GDP and agricultural output are exogenous
	– sectoral-specific total factory productivity growth rate are endogenous
	– 3 per cent growth rate of import quota for goods subjected to quantitative restriction (rice, wheat, corn, cotton, wool, vegetable oil, sugar, petroleum refining, automobiles)
	– exogenous export quota growth for textiles and apparel
	– textiles: 5.0 per cent apparel: 6.2 per cent (annual average)
	– all tax rates are fixed at their base year (2000) level
	– balance of payment gradually declines to 30 per cent of base-year level in 2010
E2	*Tariff reduction and quotas elimination on industrial products*
	– an average 55 per cent cut of 2000 tariff level from 2000–8, based on the nominal tariff schedule in China–US agreement
	– phased elimination of import quotas on petroleum refining and automobiles from 2000–5
	– initial quota in 2000 – *petroleum refining*: 27.6 billion yuan; *automobiles*: 496.8 billion yuan
	– annual growth rate of quota from 2000–5 *petroleum refining*: 15 per cent; *automobiles*: 15 per cent
E3	*Agricultural trade liberalization*

Introduction of TRQ system

	initial quota in 2000	annual growth rate of quota
rice	0.857	18.9 per cent
wheat	1.158	7.2 per cent
corn	0.325	12.5 per cent
cotton	1.046	4.7 per cent
wool	0.635	4.5 per cent
vegetable oil	10.428	14.5 per cent
sugar	1.523	8.0 per cent

– Tariff cut for other agricultural goods, based on the nominal tariff schedule in China–US agreement

E4	*Phase out of MFA*
	– acceleration of MFA quota growth rate from 2000–4
	– zero export tax of textiles and apparel in 2005
E5	*The whole WTO accession package*
	– E2, E3 and E4 combined

China's WTO accession to see the whole effects of China's WTO accession. All the assumptions for the baseline scenario and four policy scenarios are summarized in Table 5.8.

Annex II

Controlling air pollution and saving lives in Beijing*

The 'dose-response' relationships linking atmospheric pollution to respiratory disease in Beijing have been estimated by Xu et al. (1994). Their study shows that atmospheric sulphur dioxide concentration is highly correlated with damage from respiratory disease. Recent scientific evidence provides some insight into the nature of this relationship. Sulphur dioxide and other oxides of sulphur combine with oxygen to form sulphates, and with water vapour to form aerosols of sulphurous and sulphuric acid. Such acid mists can irritate the respiratory systems of humans and animals. Therefore, a high concentration of sulphur dioxide can affect breathing, and may aggravate existing respiratory and cardiovascular diseases. Sensitive populations include children, the elderly, asthmatics and individuals with bronchitis or emphysema.

The second, and probably more significant, effect of sulphur dioxide is traceable to the impact of fine particulates (less than two microns) on mortality and morbidity. A review of recent evidence by USEPA suggests that fine particulates are the source of the worst health damage from air pollution. In the case of China, there is reason to believe that from 30 to 40 per cent of fine particulates are in the form of sulphates from sulphur dioxide emissions.

In 1993, Beijing had a population of approximately 11 120 000; the mortality rate was approximately 0.611 per cent; total deaths were approximately 68 000; and total sulphur dioxide emissions were approximately 366 000 tons (of which 204 000 were from industry). From that base, a decrease of 1000 tons in sulphur dioxide emissions decreases total emissions by $1/366 \times 100$ per cent. An independent econometric analysis of the relationship between emissions and air pollution in the cities of China predicts an associated decrease of $0.51 \times 1/366 \times 100$ per cent in the ambient sulphur dioxide concentration of Beijing. Applying the Beijing 'dose-response' result of Xu et al. to the new concentration, an estimated saving of 10.4 lives per year is obtained. Dividing both elements by ten yields a useful round number for policy discussion: one life saved per 100 tons abated annually.

(*Source*: Dasgupta, S., Wang H. and Wheeler D. (1997))

Notes

1 The CGE modelling is part of the UNIDO project 'Evaluation and Adjustment of China's Sustainable Industrial Planning and Policies (US/CPR/96/108)' which was started in April 1999 funded by the government of The Netherlands. The objective of the UNIDO project is to enhance the capacity of the Department of Development Planning in the State Development Planning Commission and other government institutions to design, formulate, implement, monitor and revise industrial policies to enhance the contribution of industry to sustainable development. The projections of the CGE modelling are based on work for this project done by the Development Research Center of the State Council (Zhai and Li, 2000).

2 This CGE modelling effort takes into account structural changes (sectoral distribution of output) only in the short-to-medium-term. It does not take into account longer-term productivity growth because the modelling effort is based on fixed technological coefficients. To take productivity growth into account would require making assumptions about changes in technological coefficients, which was beyond the scope of this exercise.

3 One might question the consistency between Tables 5.1 and 5.2, where Table 5.1 shows a significant growth in aggregate terms, while the breakdown in Table 5.2 shows minuses and pluses. They are consistent if one looks at the implicit sectoral weights in Table 5.2, where output variations are provided not only by percentage, but also in billion RMB. For instance, textiles grow by RMB 491.7 billion, a 23.4 per cent increase. This indirectly tells one that the baseline value was around RMB 400 billion. This compares, directly this time, to the decreases recorded in other sectors: paper and printing loses 'only' RMB 3.8 billion, chemicals RMB 23.6 billion, etc. Clearly, the weight of the textile sector is such that a 23.4 per cent growth there is more than sufficient to offset the contradiction in nearly all other sectors.

4 A related objection, which is not examined here, is that environmental regulation adversely affects employment as well as plant-level expenditures. A number of modelling exercises and other empirical studies undertaken by developed countries contradict that perception (Sprenger, 1997): 'The employment effects of environmental policies appear to be small, relative to total employment levels, and tend to be swamped by other, more influential changes taking place in the economy and, if anything, environmental policies have had a small net beneficial effect on employment, at least in the short and medium term.'

5 As pointed out by Nordström and Vaughan (1999), the OECD compares pollution abatement costs as a percentage of production costs, whereas the US Census Bureau compares pollution abatement costs as a percentage of the value of shipments. The two concepts are closely related because market prices (the value of shipments) in the long run tend to be reduced to the unit production costs, including a 'normal' return to capital.

6 To take the example put forward by Nordström and Vaughan (1999), the production costs of steel in the US are estimated at US$513 per ton, of which US$15 can be attributed to pollution abatement. The cost of producing steel in Mexico is estimated at US$415 per ton. Thus even if all environmental regulations were removed in the US, the production costs would still exceed the level in Mexico by US$83. That is, whatever the roots of the

competitiveness problems of the steel industry in the US, only a tiny fraction can be blamed on environmental regulations (OECD, 1997a).

7 The case studies were undertaken by UNIDO, the United Nations Conference on Trade and Development (UNCTAD) and the Economic Commission for Latin America and the Caribbean (ECLAC). The case studies covered six industrial sectors reflecting the experience of different export-oriented industrial sectors, with varying degrees of pollution intensity and firm size, in selected developing countries.

8 The present report made no effort to review the limited literature that directly addresses the impact of environmental regulations on international trade patterns. Even in the most polluting sectors that spend comparatively larger amounts to comply with environmental regulations, such as pulp and paper, petroleum products, organic and inorganic chemicals, coal mining, cement, and ferrous and non-ferrous metals, would show no discernible impact (Piritti, 1994). Contrary to common perceptions, higher environmental standards have not led to lower their international competitiveness. Little systematic relationship has been found between higher environmental standards and competitiveness in environmentally sensitive goods (those that include the highest pollution abatement and control costs).

9 Many of these difficulties could be identified and addressed if China undertook economic impact assessments when setting standards for specific industrial sectors as was done by USEPA in the 1970s. More recent analyses, such as one done for the Brazilian iron and steel industry, show differences in the sector that result from size of firm and production process technology (Barton, 1999).

10 Those interested in such matters might review 'Industrial pollution control policies in China: evaluations and recommendations' (PRCEE, 2001), 'China environmental sector update' (World Bank, 2001b) and *Greening Industry: New Roles of Communities, Markets and Governments* (World Bank, 1999).

11 OECD (1999) reviews the full range of win-win benefits that can accrue to developing countries that open their domestic markets to foreign providers of environmental services, such as pollution control. The report includes several case studies from developing countries.

References and bibliography

Alam, G. (2001), 'Acquisition of environmentally suitable technologies by China – the case of circulating fluidized bed combustion boilers', paper prepared for UNIDO project US/CPR/96/108 (Vienna, Austria: UNIDO).

Anderson, R. and Kobrin, P. (2000), 'Regulatory analysis at EPA', report prepared for the US Environmental Protection Agency (Washington, DC: USEPA).

Barton, J. (1999), 'The Brazilian iron and steel industry: environmental regulation, globalization of production and technological change', Research Paper Number 7 (Maastricht, The Netherlands, United Nations University: Institute for New Technologies).

Berkel, R. van (1996), 'Cleaner production in practice: methodology development for environmental improvement of industrial production and evolution of practical experiences', doctoral thesis (Amsterdam, The Netherlands, University of Amsterdam).

Brandon, C. and Hommen, K. (1995), *The Cost of Inaction: Valuing the Economy-wide Cost of Environmental Degradation in India*, Asia Environment Division (Washington, DC: World Bank).

China Daily (1999), 'China: Haier Group's exports soar', 19 December.

Chua, S. (1999), 'Economic growth, liberalization, and the environment: a review of the economic evidence', *Annual Review of Energy and Environment*, 24: 391–430.

Chudnovsky, D., Lugones, G. and Chidiak, M. (1995), 'Comercio internacional y medio ambiente el case Argentino' (Buenos Aires: CENIT).

Dasgupta, S., Wang, H. and Wheeler, D. (1997), 'Surviving success: policy reform and the future of industrial pollution in China', World Bank Development Research Group, Working Paper No. 1856 (Washington, DC: World Bank).

Démurger, S. (2000), *Economic Opening and Growth in China*, Development Center Studies (Paris: OECD).

Garcia, D. (1994), *Reconciliation of Trade and Environmental Policies: the Case of Colombia*, UNCTAD Case Studies (Geneva, Switzerland: UNCTAD).

Guang, X. (1997), 'An estimate of the economic consequences of environmental pollution in China', Policy Research Center of the State Environmental Protection Agency (Beijing: State Environmental Protection Administration).

Hettige, H., Martin, P., Singh, M. and Wheeler, D. (1995), 'The industrial pollution projection system', World Bank Policy Research Department, Policy Research Working Paper 1431 (Washington, DC: World Bank).

Low, P. (1992), 'Trade measures and environmental quality: the implications of Mexico's exports', in P. Low (ed.), *International Trade and the Environment*, World Bank Discussion Paper 159 (Washington, DC: World Bank).

Luken, R. (1997), 'Trade implications of international standards for environmental management systems', *Green Productivity: In Pursuit of Better Quality of Life* (Tokyo: Asian Productivity Organization), 215–24.

Margulis, S. (1996), 'Back-of-the-envelope estimates of environmental damage cost in Mexico', in P. H. May and R. Seroa da Motta (eds), *Pricing the Planet: Economic Analysis for Sustainable Development* (New York: Columbia University Press).

Nordström, H. and Vaughan, S. (1999), *Trade and Environment*, Special Studies 4 (Geneva, Switzerland: Word Trade Organization).

O'Connor, D. (1996), 'Grow now/clean later, or pursuit of sustainable development', Technical Paper No. 111 (Paris: OECD).

Organization for Economic Cooperation and Development (OECD) (1996), 'Pollution abatement and control expenditure in OECD countries', OCDE/GD (96) 50 (Paris: OECD).

—— (1997a), 'The effects of government environmental policy on costs and competitiveness: iron and steel sector', DSTI/SI/SC (97) 46 (Paris: OECD).

—— (1997b), *Reforming Environmental Regulation in OECD Countries* (Paris: OECD).

—— (1999), 'The "win-win" role of trade liberalization in promoting environmental protection and economic development', Environmental services (Paris: OECD).

Office of Management and Budget (1997), *Report to Congress on the Costs and Benefits of Federal Regulations*, 30 September 1997.

Piritti, S. (1994), 'Competitiveness and environmental standards', World Bank Policy Research Working Paper Number 1249 (Washington, DC: World Bank).

Policy Research Center for Environment and Economy (PRCEE) of China's State Environmental Protection Administration (2001), 'Industrial pollution control policies in China: evaluations and recommendations', Paper prepared for UNIDO project US/CPR/96/108 (Beijing, P. R. China, State Environmental Protection Administration).

Reppelin-Hill, V. (1999), 'Trade and environment: an empirical analysis of technology effect in the steel industry', *Journal of Environmental Economics and Management*, 38, 283–301.

Ruijters, Y. (1995), 'The relevance of environmental legislation for the transfer of environmentally sound technology: the Mexican experience', Discussion Paper 9515, Institute for New Technologies (Maastricht, The Netherlands: United Nations University).

Seroa, R. and Fernandez, A. (1996), 'Health costs associated with air pollution in Brazil', in P. H. May and R. Seroa da Motta (eds), *Pricing the Planet: Economic Analysis for Sustainable Development* (New York: Columbia University Press).

Shi, H. (2001), 'Cleaner production in the People's Republic of China', draft (Beijing, P.R. China: Center for Environmentally Sound Technology Transfer).

Sprenger, R. U. (1997), 'Environmental policies and employment' (Paris: OECD).

United Nations Conference on Trade and Development (UNCTAD) (1995), 'Effects of environmental policies, standards and regulations on market access and competitiveness, with special reference to developing countries, including the least developed among them and in light of UNCTAD empirical studies', report by the UNCTAD Secretariat, Trade and Development Board, Ad Hoc Working Group on Trade, Environment and Development (Geneva, Switzerland: UNCTAD).

United Nations Development Programme/United Nations Industrial Development Organization (UNDP/UNIDO) (1998), 'Industrial pollution reduction in Dong Nai', Final project report, DG/VIE/95/053 (Hanoi, Vietnam: UNDP).

United Nations Industrial Development Organization (UNIDO) (1995), 'Environmental policies and industrial competitiveness: are they compatible?' Background Paper for 'Global Forum on Industry: Perspectives for 2000 and Beyond', Panel IV Environmental policies and industrial competitiveness, New Delhi, India, 16–18 October 1995 (Vienna, Austria: UNIDO).

US Environmental Protection Agency (USEPA) (1997), 'The benefits and costs of the Clean Air Act, 1970 to 1990', prepared for the US Congress by Office of Air and Radiation/Office of Policy Analysis and Review and Office of Policy, Planning and Evaluation/Office of Economy and Environment (Washington, DC: USEPA).

Wiemann, J. et al. (1994), 'Ecological product standards and requirements as a new challenge for developing countries' industries and exports: the case of India's leather, textile and refrigeration industries' (Berlin: German Development Institute).

World Bank (1994), *Indonesia: Environment and Development: a World Bank Country Study* (Washington, DC: World Bank).

—— (1998), *Clear Water, Blue Skies, China's Environment in the New Century* (Washington, DC: World Bank).

—— (1999), *Greening Industry: New Roles of Communities, Markets and Governments* (New York: Oxford University Press).

—— (2001a), *Development Indicators* (Washington, DC: World Bank).

—— (2001b), 'China environmental sector update' (Washington DC: World Bank).

Xu, X. et al. (1994), 'Air pollution and daily mortality in residential areas of Beijing, China', *Archives of Environmental Health*, 49 (4), 216–22.

Zhai, F. and Li, S. (1998), 'A computable general equilibrium (CGE) model for Chinese economy', Development Research Center (Beijing, P.R. China: State Council).

—— (2000), 'China's WTO accession and implications for its regional economies', Development Research Center, Paper prepared for UNIDO project US/CPR/96/108 (Beijing, P.R. China: The State Council).

6
China and the WTO: a Developing Country Perspective

Julio J. Nogués

> 'The common task posed before all the WTO members is to make the WTO rule system equitably represent the common interests of the developed and developing countries, and to make the agreement on market opening more conducive to the economic development of the developing countries.'
>
> (Long, 2000)

These words summarize the main challenge faced by developing countries in their efforts to build a development-oriented WTO and a more balanced multilateral trading system.

This chapter is devoted to the discussion of some of the institutional contributions that China can make to the WTO as the biggest and most powerful developing country member. It can be argued that, in several specific cases to be indicated below, in defending its own interests in the WTO, China will also be defending the interests of other developing countries. In this rebalancing of forces, China will also be strengthening the trading system itself.

In order to better understand this role, it is useful to look into the rules and principles that are biased against, or contribute the least to the interests of developing countries. These are classified here under two categories: market access problems and issues related to rules and principles including participation, transparency and reciprocity.

The unbalanced multilateral trading system

Access to the markets of the developed countries: agriculture and textile products[1]

The great majority of the developing countries' exports encounter high barriers in the markets of the industrialized countries. In textiles, clothing, agriculture, furs and food products, access to the industrial countries is made difficult among other things by: (i) restrictive quotas and other non-tariff barriers (NTBs), (ii) high tariffs, (iii) peak, seasonal and specific tariffs that increase the protection granted by *ad valorem* tariffs to very high levels, and (iv) sanitary-phytosanitary barriers as well as technical regulations, many of them protectionist in character. Some of this protectionism falls heavily on developing countries including China.

Agriculture

During the first decades of the multilateral trading system that was created with the General Agreement on Tariff and Trade (GATT) in 1947, the protection granted to agriculture by industrial countries was institutionalized as a result of exemptions to some multilateral rules including those on subsidies and quotas. This institutionalization allowed the growth of agricultural protectionism that today has reached irrationally high levels. The industrial countries that actually drafted the GATT, and who more recently have also been the ones that led the creation of the WTO, promoted this institutionalization.

For example, Table 6.1 presents some of the tariff barriers implemented by the European Union (EU) in favour of several agro-industrial products. The high average and maximum tariffs illustrate the consequences of having excluded these products from the GATT rules and from the first seven rounds of multilateral trade negotiations. These rounds centred on trade barriers on manufactured products and,

Table 6.1　Agricultural protection in the EU

Chapter	Name	Average tariffs	Maximum tariffs
1	Live animals	26.2	106.0
2	Meat and meat products	33.3	236.4
4	Dairy products, etc.	40.3	146.1
7	Vegetables	12.0	140.7
8	Fruits	9.6	130.4
10	Cereals	47.3	179.7
11	Wheat and mill products	24.5	137.8
12	Seeds, etc.	2.3	67.0
15	Animal and vegetable oil and fats	8.2	89.8
16	Meat and fish preparations	18.4	50.1
19	Cereal preparations	17.9	48.5
20	Vegetable and fruit preparations	22.7	161.5

Source: WTO (2000).

as a consequence, the average tariff protecting these products in the industrial countries has declined from levels above 50 per cent in the postwar period, to around 3–5 per cent. As a consequence of this double-track liberalization process, while world trade of manufactured products has increased by around 18 times since the creation of GATT in 1947, that of agricultural products has increased by only six times.

Fifteen years ago, industrial countries promised that the trade barriers of agricultural and agro-industrial products would be reduced. In a nutshell, the agreement between industrial and developing countries for launching the Uruguay Round (UR) in 1986 was that the first would liberalize their textile and agro-industrial markets in exchange for the developing countries to negotiate in the areas that were 'new' to the multilateral system of the GATT, including services and intellectual property.

For example, on agriculture, the Ministerial Declaration of the UR asserts:

> Negotiations shall aim to achieve greater liberalization of trade in agriculture and bring all measures affecting import access and export competition under strengthened and more operationally effective GATT rules and disciplines, taking into account the general principles governing the negotiations by: (i) improving market access through inter alia, the reduction of import barriers. (Ministerial Declaration on the UR, GATT, 1986)

This promise was not kept and, as a consequence, the levels of agricultural protectionism are similar to or higher than they were before the UR. For example, the Organization for Economic Cooperation and Development (OECD) has estimated that as a percentage of agricultural income of their member countries, the level of assistance provided by numerous protectionist and subsidy policies increased from 31 per cent in 1997 to 40 per cent in 1999, that is, by 9 per cent. While this assistance declined in 2000, the OECD asserts that this reduction 'reflected international price and exchange rate movements rather than major agricultural policy changes. There were no major policy reform initiatives' (OECD, 2001).

What happened? How is it possible that some countries have a legal right to continue increasing protection and subsidies to agricultural products in spite of the promise made in 1986? In order to answer this question we have to analyze the obligations assumed by the industrial countries and the rules that guided their implementation. In the agricultural negotiations of the UR, the industrial countries committed themselves to:

• Replace NTBs with equivalent ad-valorem tariffs
• Reduce these tariffs by 36 per cent in a period of six years, and
• Reduce other programmes of assistance to agriculture

If these commitments had been implemented as understood, we should observe, having ended in 2000 the six-year implementation period, a level of agricultural protection at least 36 per cent below that observed at the conclusion of the UR. This is not the case. Why? One reason lies in the tariffication of NTBs. In spite of the fact that tariffication is a simple exercise, the substitution of NTBs by *ad valorem* tariffs was not done in an adequate manner. For example, if a country has an import quota for sugar that raises the domestic price to a level that is double the international price, the *ad valorem* equivalent tariff of the quota is 100 per cent; if it raises the domestic price by 50 per cent, the equivalent tariff is 50 per cent, etc.

Table 6.2 illustrates some examples of 'dirty tariffs' of the EU. Column 2 of each product represents the average UR *ad valorem* tariff that was notified to the WTO, and Column 1 is the 'correctly measured' *ad valorem* tariff equivalent of NTBs. It can be seen that for some products like meat and rice, a tariff reduction of 36 per cent of the base notified to the WTO, leaves the rates of protection at levels that are higher than those in place before these negotiations were initiated (Hathaway and Ingco, 1996; Ingco, 1996).[2]

Table 6.2   Dirty tariffication by the EU

	Agricultural products						
	Rice		Wheat		Cereals		Sugar	
EU	153	360.5	103.3	155.6	133	134.4	234	297

	Livestock products						
	Beef		Pork		Chicken		Dairy products	
EU	83	125.4	40	51.7	51	44.5	177	288.5

Column 1: Equivalent Tariff 1986–88.
Column 2: Tariff reported to the WTO.
Source: Hathaway and Ingco (1996).

Finally, industrial countries also enjoyed other escape valves including special safeguards for agricultural products, the choice of a base period that biases protection upward, the possibility of excluding many products from tariffication and, as seen, the possibility of granting massive amounts of subsidies (Hathaway and Ingco, 1996).[3]

So, tariffication, the reduction of tariffs by 36 per cent and other 'similar obligations' have not had any significant effect in reducing agricultural protection. Nevertheless, they served the purpose of mounting an effective public relations campaign for arguing that industrial countries were liberalizing. In practice, these commitments were 'smoke and mirrors', without positive economic effects of importance for the countries that are efficient producers of agricultural products. In fact, for some of these countries, there have been serious negative effects including those associated with international price declines leading to increasing export subsidies (Hathaway and Ingco, 1996; and Nogués, 2001).

Summing up, the Agreement on Agriculture is the only agreement in the history of the multilateral system that has legalized an increase in the protection granted to a particular economic sector by a particular group of countries. All of this occurred, as we have seen, in a very opaque manner.

Textiles and clothing

For decades, the textile and clothing industry, the other sector of significant export interest to developing countries, remained protected by industrial countries. In this case, nevertheless, the UR negotiations were more favourable for the efficient producers than was the case for the agricultural ones. According to the Agreement on Textiles and Clothing (ATC), the dismantling of the quotas of the Multi-Fibre Agreement (MFA) should be implemented in four stages: 16 per cent in 1995, 17 per cent in 1998, 18 per cent in 2002, and 49 per cent in 2005. As seen, this programme has a period of implementation of ten years that is so long that it could be asserted that the special and differential principle of the GATT and the WTO has been inverted in order to allow industrial countries more time to adapt than the time developing countries took to implement their market access concessions.

Also note that a great portion of the dismantling of the MFA will be implemented only by 2005 when 49 per cent of the quotas will be eliminated. Finally, as was the case with the Agreement on Agriculture, the ATC also includes special safeguards, which in fact have been used by industrial countries (Finger and Schuknecht, 1999). This and other loopholes imply that an important part of the 33 per cent notional liberalization that should already be implemented according to the timetables of the ATC, has in fact not occurred. On this, we can conclude that:

> Through the first two stages, which include notionally thirty-three per cent of textiles and clothing imports, the United States (US) has eliminated only one per cent of its MFA restrictions, the EU only seven per cent, Canada only fourteen per cent. Liberalization to date under the ATC has been mostly on products that were not under restraint to begin with. (Finger and Nogués, 2001).

It is important to recall that the available estimates indicate that this liberalization will also bring important benefits to industrial countries. For example, in terms of reduced costs to consumers from lower prices, for the US, the gains from liberalization of textile and clothing trade is estimated to be in the order of US\$24 billion per year (Hufbauer and Elliot, 1994).

The slow process of liberalization of textile trade, in spite of the important benefits it will bring, shows how powerful the industrial countries' textile lobby is. How many jobs could have been created and how much poverty could have been avoided in the developing countries if agricultural and textile protectionism had been dismantled by the end of the UR? Historically, China has been one of the countries most affected by the MFA quotas. For example, Hertel et al. (1996) have estimated that the dismantling of these quotas will increase the aggregate output of the textile and clothing sector of China by 8 per cent and 59 per cent respectively. For this country, exports of these products would increase by 14 per cent and 59 per cent respectively. Clearly, the economic and social consequences of the slow process of dismantling the MFA are serious.

Although China was excluded from the benefits derived from the ATC, upon entry to the WTO it will acquire the right to participate in the benefits of this liberalization and will begin internalizing significant gains from this liberalization. For example, Ianchovichina and Martin (2001) have recently estimated that, between 1995 and 2005, China's share in world output of textiles and clothing will increase from 7 per cent to 20 per cent, and from 20 per cent to 47 per cent respectively. These would represent significant changes in a short period of time.

Imbalance of the UR

The agriculture and textile negotiations are salient examples of the imbalance of the UR, but there were other negotiations that deepened this result.

Access to markets

The failure of the UR in opening up rich countries' markets for important products produced competitively by the developing countries was perhaps the most significant negative result of these negotiations for them. Given this outcome, it is not surprising to observe the results summarized in Figure 6.1.[4] This shows that while concessions given and received by industrial countries were approximately equal, developing countries implemented tariff cuts that were much deeper than those given to their exports by other countries. These average tariff cuts encompass all the results of the UR including those implemented by the ATC. The imbalance for the developing countries presented in Figure 6.1 is a landmark in the multilateral system. The history of the first seven rounds of these negotiations was one of approximate balance between concessions given and received by different countries that participated actively.

Figure 6.1   The UR: access to markets

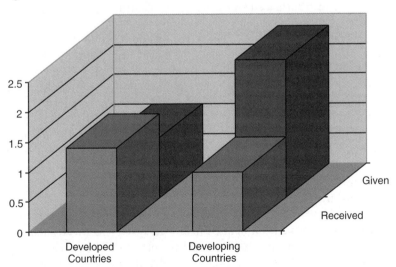

Source: Finger and Schuknecht (1999).

Finally, I would like to note that while developing countries have already implemented most or all of their market access commitments, industrial countries are still to implement important liberalization measures, including most of the dismantling of the MFA. Summing up, in the market access negotiations, the principle of special and differential treatment was inverted, to allow industrial countries to have more time to implement their obligations than developing countries.

Other topics: Trade-Related Industrial Property Rights (TRIPs) and services

The imbalance of the UR in market access for trade in goods is deepened by concessions given by the developing countries in intellectual property and services. This is so because it is industrial countries that have a clear comparative advantage in producing innovations and in supplying the most important services that were negotiated.

TRIPs

Among the topics covered by the Agreement on Trade-Related Aspects of Intellectual Property Rights, pharmaceutical drugs merit special consideration. The patenting of these drugs was a concession extracted from many developing countries under the threat of retaliation or 'aggressive unilateralism' as trade economists have called these actions (Bagwhati and Patrick, 1990). It is also important to underline that the patenting of pharmaceutical drugs was an area negotiated without knowledge regarding the possible economic and social effects that this policy would have (Nogués, 1993). For example, while the economic evaluation of a tariff only requires knowledge of the elasticity of supply and demand, there is no solid theory for analyzing the economic effects of patents or other forms of intellectual property. Under these circumstances, there cannot be transparency in the negotiations.

What effects have TRIPs had? One consequence is that in some illnesses like AIDS, the price effects of patents granted to the relevant pharmaceutical drugs are so high as to exclude most people from having access to these medicines. While tariff reductions lower prices, stronger intellectual property 'rights' increase the prices of products protected by them.

The complaints of the international community regarding the prices of these drugs have been of such magnitude that the governments of the industrial countries have started to react in order to reduce the negative effects of TRIPs. For example, some of these countries, including the EU, are asking their pharmaceutical companies to sell drugs to the poor countries at reduced prices. Thus, in a note from Brussels, the EU has indicated that it is seeking

> ...the support of the pharmaceutical industry in order to make essential medicines available to developing countries at the lowest possible prices... (http://europa.eu.int/comm/trade)

The respect for intellectual property rights imposed by industrial countries on many developing countries contrasts with their own historical experience. Industrial countries adopted patenting only when their governments concluded that the time had come to act on behalf of their innovating companies. For example, in the following countries, the introduction of patents for pharmaceutical drugs occurred in the indicated years: France: 1960; Germany: 1968; Japan: 1976; Switzerland: 1977; Italy: 1978 and Spain in the decade of the 1980s. In these countries, the unforced introduction of patents consolidated their pharmaceutical industries. In contrast to this experience, in the countries that have been 'forced' to introduce this policy, the evidence shows that their domestic pharmaceutical companies are disappearing (Nogués 2001).

In addition to the effects of stronger intellectual property rights on prices, the assumed obligations in the TRIPs imply massive transfers of rents from the producers and consumers in developing countries to the owners of intellectual property.[5] In some countries, there is also some evidence of net outflows of foreign direct investment (FDI) as well as an increase in imports of pharmaceutical products (Finger and Nogués, 2001).

So, the TRIPs is an agreement of the UR that has generated and continues to generate serious multilateral frictions. The recent adoption of a more conciliatory position by industrial countries will probably facilitate a more constructive dialogue with developing countries. But for the time being, this softer position appears to be more of a patchwork than a serious multilateral reassessment of the development effects of TRIPs. One lesson is that WTO negotiations on new topics should not be undertaken without serious economic and social analysis of possible impacts and China is a country that can impose significant pressures for this to happen.

Services

In the area of services, the developing countries also gave important concessions (Hoekman and Kostecki, 1996). In most of the services negotiated under the UR Agreement on Services, it is the industrial countries that have a clear comparative advantage in supplying them. Note for example, that in the great majority of public services that have become privatized during the last 15 years or so, the buyers have been investors and companies from the industrial countries. Binding concessions of 'commercial presence' in these services by developing countries was an important objective of the industrial countries in the UR. The bad sides of these negotiations were certainly not the developing countries' efforts to attract capital to their service industries. The bad side is that most of the concessions given by them were unrequited by industrial countries.

During the UR, the typical developing country gave important concessions in market access, in intellectual property and in services, among others. In return, market access concessions given by industrial countries were usually of lower economic value and variable from region to region. One way of assessing these regional differences is by noting that while the Latin American region, an important agricultural producer, received concessions covering 25 per cent of its exports, the Asian countries received concessions that cover approximately 50 per cent (Finger et al., 1996). The difference is explained by the agricultural negotiations in relation to other market access negotiations. The developing countries with more diversified export structures like those of East and South Asia, received concessions that were relatively more important.

Unlike other developing countries whose export structures remain heavily concentrated in primary and agro-industrial products, China has undergone an important process of diversification. In this way, China has been able to reduce the vulnerabilities associated with important 'pockets' of high protectionism in the international markets particularly in agricultural goods. Nevertheless, China has a significant service sector and its technological-intensive industries must remain alert to demands by existing multinational companies (MNCs) for extending and increasing the strength of 'intellectual property legislation' provided by the TRIPs. These demands that go well beyond the TRIPs 'obligations', have actually been put forward by the US in the negotiations of the Free Trade Agreement of the Americas (FTAA).

Development and implementation costs

Finger and Schuler (2000) argue that in contrast to tariff changes that do not imply implementation costs, many of the new multilateral agreements including the TRIPs, the Sanitary and Phytosanitary (SPS)

Agreement and the Agreement on Customs Valuation require millions of dollars. They also argue that for some countries, implementation costs can be above their combined budgets for health and education. Given their state of development and limited resources, these investments are not a priority and yet, according to these WTO agreements, they are obligatory.

Again, we observe that many agreements were negotiated and accepted without taking into account the costs and problems of implementation that the poorest countries would be confronting. For the industrial countries, these agreements do not have implementation costs because they are simply a replica of their actual standards. Essentially, what happened is that these countries said, 'This is the manner in which we administer these topics and these will be the new international legal standards.' The absence of analysis and discussion regarding the possibilities of the developing countries for implementing these standards has had two effects: (i) the creation of agreements that are not of development priority and (ii) a likely waste of resources by poor countries as they invest in the implementation of these agreements.

Developing countries face other related problems that increase the costs of doing business with industrial countries. One of these is associated with the rapid growth of sanitary, phytosanitary and technical standards (OECD, 1999). Even if they undertake the necessary investments mentioned above, developing countries will remain unsure as to their returns. For example, when some of their products are exported, the importing countries often require costly tests and certifications to ensure that they meet 'international standards'. If the newly created or newly refurbished developing countries' standards organizations are slow to gain international reputation, as will most likely be the case, the tests will have to be made by importing countries at an additional cost.[6] It is of interest also to note that developing countries' weak scientific base is unlikely to have the strength needed to challenge unreasonable standards set by countries with a powerful scientific base. Recent research shows, for example, the damage on Africa's exports that has been inflicted by setting a standard for aflatoxin residue that is much more stringent than the one suggested by Codex Alimentarius (Otsuki et al., 2001).

Developing countries face two challenges. First, they should attempt to renegotiate some WTO agreements including the Agreement on the Application of SPS Measures. For example, precautionary measures allowed by the SPS have been costly and usually applied discretionally

(Wilson, 2001). Second, they should also participate more actively in the organizations setting international standards such as the International Standard Organization (ISO). The objective here is that by enhancing this participation, standards will be truly international and not only the reflection of preferences set by those countries that have a commanding position in these organizations. For the time being, participation by developing countries in these organizations remains minimal and existing standards tend to reflect more the development levels of industrial countries (WTO, 1997). Given China's powerful scientific base, its influence can shift the criteria used in the international standard-setting organizations so that they reflect its needs appropriately which, in turn, are likely to resemble the needs of other developing countries more than those of industrial countries.

Other problems

In the category of 'other problems', there are two that have imposed heavy costs on China and other developing countries: (i) regulations against unfair competition and (ii) the costs of complying with the rules of the rules-based system.

Unfair competition

Several of the industrial countries' mechanisms against unfair competition (dumped and subsidized imports) are extremely protectionist and sufficiently complex as to impose very high costs on developing countries. For example, while some countries adhere to the principle of the 'lesser duty to overcome injury', other countries like the US apply anti-dumping and countervailing duties that are equivalent to the full dumping or subsidy margins. Most of the time, these margins are higher than necessary to cover for the 'injury' that has been found to be caused by dumped or subsidized imports. Furthermore, given the potential high costs of these measures, developing country exporters or their governments may be unwise to save on legal costs by, say, not hiring a US-based lawyer. Typical legal fees for these cases are in the order of US$400 000 to US$500 000 and often developing country exporters, particularly if they are small and acting on their own, find it difficult, if not impossible, to pay these fees.

China is among the countries most affected by measures against unfair competition imposed by WTO members and in particular, by industrial countries (Baldwin, 1998). The bias of these regimes against China has been such that special and more protectionist procedures, particularly for estimating inflated margins of dumping, have been developed to deal with imports from this country. In fact, because China has not been a member of the WTO, some countries apply measures and administrative procedures that are not consistent with the relevant WTO agreements (Agreement on Implementation of Article VI of the GATT 1994 and Agreement on Subsidies and Countervailing Measures).

Immediately upon entry, China has two options: to argue in the WTO in favour of a change of multilateral rules against unfair competition in order to make them more pro-competitive, or to follow a protectionist path by replicating, say, mechanisms like those used by the US. The gains to be reaped if China chooses the first alternative are significant.

Rules of the game and participation

It is often argued that one of the positive aspects of the WTO is that it represents a 'rules-based system'. Except for a few cases such as the Plurilateral Agreements, most of the rules apply to all countries independently of their development stage. But not all countries have the same capacity to play the game by following these rules. First, going back to the legal costs associated with unfair trade cases, recall that if these resources have to be borrowed, interest rates in developing countries are much higher than in industrial countries. On the other hand, the cost of legal fees in developing countries is lower and the burden on exporters who engage in trade cases there, particularly if they are from industrial countries, is much lower. This is one example where the costs of complying with the 'rules-based system' are not proportional to ability to pay. Likewise, developing countries may have to meet high legal fees in cases brought against them to the WTO Dispute Settlement Mechanism (DSM).

There is also evidence of weak participation by developing countries in international trade negotiations, sometimes caused by lack of resources and sometimes by explicit discriminatory treatment. For example, in the UR, a group of around 20 poor countries did not even have an observer during the Geneva-based negotiations (Blackhurst et al., 1999). These countries were asked to sign the UR agreements without them knowing what were the implications for their societies. They were also promised technical assistance that would explain to them what the UR meant, but the WTO has never had an adequate technical assistance budget.

Third, in addition to the 'resource problems' of the poor countries, there is evidence that in important decision-making processes, industrial countries and big emerging countries prefer to negotiate without the participation of the smaller and economically less relevant countries. A salient example of this occurred at the Seattle Meeting where many developing countries were not invited to the 'green room' where some of the most important discussions took place (Odell, 2000). China could demand that the WTO consider strengthening the provision of legal advice to safeguard the exports of the poorest countries. China can also defend its interests by demanding the creation of mechanisms that allow full participation of developing countries in the decision-making process of the WTO.

Rules and principles for strengthening the multilateral trading system

Reciprocity principle

As mentioned, up to the UR, the principle of reciprocity and balanced multilateral negotiations was respected. As a consequence, there is no historical evidence of countries participating actively in these negotiations, and walking away with a sense of disillusionment. This high degree of achievement covered the first seven rounds of multilateral trade negotiations, that is, close to 50 years of GATT rules and principles. This is in sharp contrast to the very unbalanced UR outcome and the tensions that it has unleashed.

The unbalanced UR outcome can be traced back to some structural weakness of developing countries and to a greater influence of interest groups in the WTO countries. Upon joining the WTO, China can play a significant role in bringing back the reciprocity principle to where it was. This principle, first stated in the preamble to the GATT and then picked up again in Article XXVIII bis states that for achieving trade liberalization member countries should enter into:

> reciprocal and mutually advantageous arrangements directed to the substantial reduction of tariffs and other barriers to trade and to the elimination of discriminatory treatment in international commerce (preamble to the GATT).

The principle was also repeated in the UR Ministerial Declaration, and it is repeated over and over again, but the problem is that developing countries have not yet found ways of ensuring that all WTO members follow it. In this case, the role of China will be of the greatest significance, particularly if there is another multilateral round. Long reminds us that, it has taken more than 15 years to negotiate China's accession to the WTO. Many things must have gone on behind this 'Guinness record', as he calls this long journey, and one of them has been the strong stand on the 'condition that China will only enter into the WTO as a developing country' and that it has been 'by no means easy to make the decision-makers or negotiation representatives in the Western countries understand the situation in China' (Long, 2000). Clearly, China has stood firm by its position and interests, and this strength is what developing countries need in order to avoid another unbalanced multilateral trade negotiation.

Transparency

While the degree of compliance with the reciprocity principle can be quantified, the extent to which transparency is present in a negotiation is a matter of judgement. There is no manifest evidence that the countries that participated actively in the first seven rounds of multilateral negotiations felt transparency lacking. Compare this with the dirty agricultural tariffs, or with the absence of knowledge regarding the likely effects of TRIPs, or with the loopholes allowing a slow implementation of the ATC, or with the lack of knowledge regarding the implementation problems of several UR agreements.

Much of the opacity in the UR has damaged the WTO badly. Again, this is in contrast to the first seven rounds of multilateral trade negotiations under the aegis of the GATT. The fact that during the UR most developing countries attended the meetings does not imply that the negotiations were transparent. Most of the developing countries sitting at the table were negotiating without relevant knowledge of the economic impacts of the many areas that were included in the UR; that is, they were negotiating blindfolded.

Transparency was a goal included in the Ministerial Declaration that launched the UR:

> Negotiations shall be conducted in a transparent manner, and consistent with the objectives and commitments agreed in this Declaration and with the principles of the General Agreement in order to ensure mutual advantage and increased benefits to all participants (Ministerial Declaration on the UR, GATT, 1986).

Again, the problem is that the promise was not kept. In its long negotiating process, China has been very careful not to upset the equilibrium between domestic and international interests. The negotiating stance of developing countries can certainly be strengthened by studies quantifying the balance of concessions given and received in different areas.

Participation

The trading system will not become more balanced and less discriminatory unless there is increased participation by developing countries and an understanding by industrial countries that this is important. As mentioned, several multilateral rules only reflect the development stage of the industrial countries. Enhanced participation by developing countries should help make the rules reflect different stages of development, not only that of industrial countries. Take the functioning of the customs offices of member countries: the WTO Agreement on Customs Valuation only cares about valuation when in fact, the problems faced by the customs of developing countries are severe and cover many other areas. 'One rule fits all' is not an appropriate development concept. Multilateral and regional development banks have long ago realized that this was the case. As a consequence, these institutions have developed a myriad of loan products whose interest costs and repayment periods vary by type of objective (balance of payments, structural adjustment and sectoral loans), and by the income levels (the lower the income level the longer the repayment period and/or the interest rate), achieved by the borrowing countries. It is time now for the WTO to follow the path of these other organizations; China could help.

Conclusions

China's entry to the WTO is a historical landmark of the multilateral trading system created after the second World War. China joins as a developing country and its sheer economic size will surely add weight to this group of countries in their dealings with the developed ones. How China performs from day one will determine the nature of the future WTO as an international organization. China's entry to the WTO takes place at a very particular juncture in the history of the trading system. The UR opened a divide between those countries that have and those that have not obtained reciprocal access to foreign markets. It also opened a divide between those countries that can and those that cannot fully play by the rules. The difference between them is not a matter of willingness to participate in the trading system, but a matter of different stages of development and capacities. The WTO has to be reformed and a new multilateral round is necessary, if only to close the divide opened by the UR. Both of these are necessary if China's goal is to 'make the WTO system equitably represent the common interests of the developed and developing countries' (Long, 2000).

The following are the areas where China could make the most significant development-oriented contributions, while strengthening some rules and principles that would recreate a more equitable multi-lateral trading system.

Negotiating power and the gains from worldwide growth

As said, the UR entailed a major change to the trading system created in the late 1940s. During the first 50 years or so, the smaller and less powerful countries remained protected by basic principles including transparency, reciprocity, most-favoured-nation, and national treat-ment. Under these rules and principles, the achievements of the GATT trading system remain remarkable, including a far-reaching liberaliza-tion that resulted in a sustained process of high export and per capita GDP growth rates of the active participants to the negotiations. This early 'encompassing globalization process' compares with what we have seen during the last 15 years or so, where only a handful of devel-oping countries that participated in the UR are closing their per capita income differentials with the average industrial countries (IMF, 2000).

One possible reason could be that the first seven multilateral rounds under the aegis of the GATT only covered barriers to trade in goods. In addition to the respect for the basic principles listed above, the formu-las used for negotiating the reduction of barriers were quite even-handed (Hoekman and Kostecki, 1995). A salient example of this is found in the Tokyo Round, where countries agreed to apply the same tariff-reduction formula to their tariff structures. Under this arrange-ment, neither size nor power was used to pressure the less powerful members; the agreement was that everyone applied the same formula and everyone could quantify the likely economic effects of applying it in a very precise manner. These were the days of maximum trans-parency and maximum reciprocity.

The principle of reciprocity was created by the Reciprocal Trade Agreement Act of 1932, passed by the US Congress (Destler, 1992). Over time, the power of special-interest lobbies grew, to the point that in the late 1980s the US Congress approved 301 and 'Special 301', which represents a clear benefit in favour of the international pharma-ceutical companies and other powerful pressure groups (Baghwati and Patrick, 1990). The retaliatory threats made with the backing of the

301 legislation and Special 301 have caused much tension and damage to the trading system.

The agenda of the GATT was driven by the aim of restoring a healthy world economy after a war had devastated it. The agenda of the UR was driven by interest groups and, therefore, it is not adequate for creating the conditions for a healthy and balanced world economy.

First conclusion: it is necessary to ensure that in the next round of multilateral negotiations, the powerful rent-seeking lobbies do not push the powerful countries to negotiate in favour of private interests that are divorced from the national interest and from the objective of a more equitable multilateral system.

Multilateral rules and development stages

As mentioned, the rules of the WTO do not reflect the stages of development of many of its members. The challenge of adjusting the underlying biases goes beyond the special and differential principle. The rules of the WTO are more rigid than those of the GATT, and in a development perspective this is a regression. For example, when new negotiating topics were introduced in the Kennedy and Tokyo Rounds, the agreements reached among a few members were not compulsory for the others. These were the years of the GATT Codes that included optional rules of conduct. For example, most developing country members were not signatories to the Anti-dumping Code and the Code of Subsidies and Countervailing Measures.

Compare this flexibility with the agreements of the UR adopted as a single undertaking. Under this format, any country had to accept the whole UR package of agreements and become a member of the WTO, or refuse to sign and remain outside of the WTO and also of the GATT that was submerged into the new organization. The single undertaking put countries in a straitjacket: either they accepted everything, or else become isolated.

Second conclusion: the WTO has to be reformulated so that it is more representative of needs and capacities associated with very different development stages. The old GATT found ways to do this and in the light of recent experience, members have to reassess the wisdom of reincorporating something like the GATT Code system or similarly oriented alternatives.

Transparency in multilateral negotiations

The next multilateral round should be characterized by negotiating rules that ensure the highest levels of transparency and reciprocity. Opaque negotiations like those that characterized many UR agreements cannot be repeated. The factors that explain results like the dirty agricultural tariffs and loopholes that have allowed industrial countries to implement an unexpectedly slow dismantling of the MFA should be extirpated from the WTO negotiations.

Third conclusion: the problem is not to launch a new round promising transparency because this already happened in the UR without results. The fundamental challenge is that this promise be kept, perhaps by creating a mechanism like a transparency surveillance body.

Reciprocity in multilateral trade negotiations

The greatest economic harm done by the UR to developing countries originates in the huge imbalance between the concessions they gave and those they received. This cannot be repeated. Indeed, from the broken promise of the UR, in the next round, developing countries have a 'right' to demand a surplus outcome in their favour. Where should this surplus come from? Given that in the areas of services and intellectual property the comparative advantage is with the developed countries, a surplus in favour of developing countries should come primarily from enhanced market access for trade in goods.

China has completed its accession negotiations and has agreed to implement significant liberalization measures. By acceding to the WTO, in a next round, China can play a crucial leading role in demanding that the reciprocity principle be fully respected.

Fourth conclusion: in the new multilateral round, it is necessary to ensure that each country understands well the likely consequences of what it will be signing. This could be done for example by allowing countries the opportunity to complete all necessary analysis for ensuring that the round provides benefits to their societies. When the completion of these analyses indicates a significant imbalance for some countries, then the negotiations should be reopened to ensure that all countries come out of negotiations with a sense that a balanced outcome has finally been achieved. If this is not acceptable, countries should stand firm in defending their rights and be ready to block the adoption of any proposal that they conclude is not in their interests.

Notes

1 We recognize that there are access barriers to the markets of the developing countries. Nevertheless, the purpose here is to focus on industrial countries where the exports of some crucial developing countries´products confront the highest barriers and consequently, where they have the greatest potential for growth.

2 It is of interest to recall that at the UR there was a document establishing the correct way by which an NTB should be tariffed. This document was titled *Modalities for the Establishment of Specific Binding Commitments Under the Reform Program* (GATT, 1993). Because this document is not part of the legal texts, those countries that are affected by dirty tariffs cannot bring industrial countries to the Dispute Settlement Mechanism of the WTO. This was another way by which industrial countries could elude their commitment to reduce protection on agriculture and agro-based industrial production.

3 But if export subsidies are prohibited according to the WTO rules, how can industrial countries continue subsidizing their agricultural exports? Very simply, by adapting the WTO Agreement on Subsidies and Countervailing Measures to their needs. Therefore Article 3 of this Agreement that deals with prohibited export subsidies, starts by saying: 'Except as provided in the Agreement on Agriculture, the following subsidies, within the meaning of Article 1, shall be prohibited...' In this very simple way, industrial countries institutionalized export subsidies to fit their agricultural objectives that are prohibited for other products and services.

4 The fact that the average tariffs of industrial countries are lower than those of developing countries is unrelated to the issue of exchanging market access concessions in trade negotiations. The point is that developing countries' UR concessions implied greater reductions of developing countries' import prices and, therefore, facilitated industrial countries'exports to their markets more than the other way around.

5 In the case of Argentina, the rent transfer is estimated to be in the order of US$400 million per year (Nogués, 2001).

6 It is of interest to note that international standards are not truly international, as many developing countries participate only marginally if at all in their development. For example, in the ISO the share of staff from developing countries is around 5 per cent of the total (WTO, 1997).

References and bibliography

Baghwati, J. and Patrick, H. (eds) (1990), *Aggressive Unilateralism: America's 301 Trade Policy and the World Trading System* (Ann Arbor: University of Michigan Press).

Baldwin, R. (1998), 'Imposing multilateral discipline on administered protection', in Anne O. Krueger (ed.), *The WTO as an International Trade Organization* (Chicago: University of Chicago Press).

Blackhurst, R., Lyakurwa, B. and Oyejide, A. (1999), *Improving African Participation in the WTO*, mimeo (Geneva: WTO).

Destler, I. (1992), *American Trade Politics* (Washington DC: Institute for International Economics).

Finger, J. M. and Nogués, J.J. (2001), 'Unbalanced WTO negotiations: the new areas in future negotiations', *The World Economy* (forthcoming).

Finger, J. M. and Schuler, P. (2000), 'Implementation of UR commitments: the development challenge', *The World Economy*, April.

Finger, J. M. and Schuknecht, L. (1999), 'Market access advances and retreats: the UR and beyond', mimeo (Washington DC: World Bank).

Finger, J. M., Ingco, M. D. and Reincke, U. (1996), *The UR: Statistics on Tariff Concessions Given and Received* (Washington DC: World Bank).

GATT (1986), *UR Ministerial Declaration* (Geneva: GATT).

—— (1993), *Modalities for the Establishment of Specific Binding Commitments Under the Reform Program,* MTN.GNG/MA/W/24 (Geneva: GATT).

Hathaway, D. and Ingco, M. (1996), 'Agricultural liberalization and the UR,' in Martin and Winters (eds) (1996).

Hertel, T., Martin, W. et al. (1996), 'Liberalizing manufactures trade in a changing world economy', in Martin and Winters (eds) (1996).

Hoekman, B. and Kostecki, M. (1995), *The Political Economy of the World Trading System* (Oxford: Oxford University Press).

—— (1996), 'Assessing the General Agreement on Trade in Services', in Martin and Winters (eds) (1996).

Hufbauer, G. and Elliot, K. (1994), *Measuring the Costs of Protection in the United States* (Washington DC: Institute for International Economics).

Ianchovichina, E. and Martin, W. (2001), 'Trade liberalization in China's accession to WTO', mimeo (Washington DC: World Bank).

Ingco, M. (1996), *Agricultural Trade Liberalization in the UR: One Step Forward, One Step Back?,* The World Economy.

International Monetary Fund (2000), *World Economic Outlook* (Washington DC: IMF).

Long, Y. (2000), 'Opportunities for further cooperation between China and other developing countries', paper presented to UNIDO's Asia-Pacific Regional Forum on Industrial Development (Shanghai).

Martin, W. and Winters, A. L. (eds) (1996), *The UR and the Developing Countries* (Cambridge: Cambridge University Press).

Nogués, J. J. (1993), 'Social costs and benefits of introducing patent protection for pharmaceutical drugs in developing countries', *The Developing Economies,* March.

—— (2001), 'El desbalance de la Rueda Uruguay: consecuencias para la Argentina', in De Pablo, J. C., Dornbusch, R. and Nogués, J. J. (2001), *La Globalización, la Argentina y Cada Uno de Nosotros* (Buenos Aires: Consejo Empresario Argentino).

Odell, J. (2000), *The Seattle Impasse and its Implications for the World Trade Organization,* presented at the Conference on the World Trading System Post Seattle organized by CEPR/ECARES/World Bank (Brussels).

OECD (1999), *An Assesment of the Costs for International Trade in Meeting Regulatory Requirements* (Paris: OECD).

—— (2001), *Agricultural Policies in OECD Countries: Monitoring and Evaluation 2000* (Paris: OECD).

Otsuki, T., Wilson, J. and Sewadeh, M. (2001), 'Saving two in a billion: a case study to quantify the trade effects of food safety standards', mimeo (Washington DC: World Bank).

Wilson, J. (2001), 'Bridging the standard divide: recommendations for reform from a development perspective', mimeo (Washington DC: World Bank), February.

World Trade Organization (1995), *The Results of the UR of Multilateral Trade Negotiations: the Legal Text* (Geneva: WTO).
—— (1997), *Triennial Review of the Agreement on Technical Barriers to Trade* (Geneva: WTO).
—— (2000), *Trade Policy Review of the EU*, WT/TPR/S/72 (Geneva: WTO).

7

Implications of China's Entry into the WTO in the Field of Intellectual Property Rights

Long Yongtu

P33 F14
019 034

No area has taken such a prominent place in China's protracted negotiations to accede to the World Trade Organization (WTO) as that of Intellectual Property Rights (IPRs).

In the final document of the Working Party Report on China's accession, out of 343 paragraphs, 55 paragraphs covering 15 pages are devoted to an extensive treatment of the trade-related intellectual property (TRIP) regime. This shows that both China and its negotiation partners believe IPRs is an important issue in the context of China's participation in the multilateral trading system.

Background

To start with, the Chinese government had made the protection of IPRs an essential component of its reform and opening-up policy and of the creation of a socialist legal system. The formulation of laws and regulations in this field can be traced back to the late 1970s, when China initiated the historic process of reform and opening up. Since then, China has joined almost all the relevant international conventions and has taken an open approach towards exchange and cooperation with many countries in the world. As a result, China, a developing country, has already achieved the world standard in creating a legal system for IPRs.

Both the current Director-General of the World Intellectual Property Organization (WIPO) as well as his predecessors have acknowledged that China had achieved this goal within two decades while the developed countries took over 100 years. It is this background that ensured that Chinese negotiators would not encounter serious difficulties in their WTO negotiations concerning IPR issues.

Comprehensive commitments

To honour the commitments made in the negotiations, upon accession the National People's Congress of China has introduced amendments to the patent, copyright and trademark laws so that they fully comply with the TRIPs agreement. The Working Party Report cites the many comprehensive commitments China has made in the following areas: copyright protection; trademarks including service marks; geographical indications, including appellations of origin; industrial designs; patent; plant variety protection; layout designs of integrated circuits as well as requirements on undisclosed information, including trade secrets and text data.

China has also agreed with its trading partners on the issue of enforcement, which includes civil judicial procedures and remedies, administrative procedures and remedies, special border measures and criminal procedures.

We believe that there have never been such detailed provisions in the document of accession of any other WTO member. The result of the WTO negotiations on IPRs proves once again that the Chinese government is serious about its commitments on the protection of IPRs and is determined to create legal administrative and judicial frameworks to enforce the relevant IPR laws and regulations.

Implementation hurdles

However, as IPRs are such a complicated issue, there is still a long way to go for China to implement all the relevant laws and regulations. China, like many other developing countries still has to face many conceptual issues regarding the protection of IPRs. Here are a few cases:

1. Many people in China still believe that the protection of IPRs is in essence in the interest of developed countries, especially their large transnational corporations, since they control over 80 per cent of the patent, copyright and know-how rights worldwide. Therefore, they believe, emphasis on the enforcement of the relevant laws and regulations aims to preserve the vested interest of the privileged people in the West.

2. Some people consider that the provisions of some international conventions and treaties, including the TRIPs agreement, are not well balanced. The current debate in the WTO on TRIPs and public health is a case in point. It is difficult to strike a balance between the patent rights and the right of the poor to access basic life-saving drugs. Many believe that developing countries need a longer transitional period for the implementation of TRIPs.

3. Some Chinese have even complained that, historically, many developing countries, and particularly China, made great contributions by introducing scientific and technological breakthroughs (such as China's four great inventions: gunpowder, the compass, typography and paper-making); but nobody ever considered that patent fees should be paid to the Chinese for these inventions. Even though there is a flavour of bitter humour in this attitude, there clearly exists an strong undertone which suggests strong resistance to the enforcement of IPRs in developing countries that have little intellectual property at hand to protect.

However, the Chinese government has taken a strategic stand to address the protection of IPRs. It fully realizes that any shortsightedness has to be overcome for the long-term benefit of China.

Rationale of a strategic choice

China must be firm and determined in the field of protection of IPRs even though it has to pay a high cost at this stage. China has made this difficult strategy choice to comply with the TRIPs agreement for the following four considerations.

Firstly, China has made it its national policy 'to develop China through scientific and technological advancement'. We know that if China does not develop its own patents, copyrights and trademarks it will forever trail behind the developed countries and will never become a major economic power.

The consensus is that new technology developments will not be commercialized without IPR protection. This issue has some special characteristics in China, which distinguish it from many other countries. It has a huge domestic market. It has a sound basis for technology development, including scientific and technological infrastructure and human talent. To protect IPRs means, in the first place, to protect China's own IPRs. Take software, for example. China has already developed its own software in Chinese characters, which has a market of 1.3 billion Chinese, not to mention those Chinese in Taiwan Province of China, Hong Kong SAR, China and Macao as well as the descendants of Chinese in other countries. If we do not protect software in Chinese characters, the software in Chinese will never reach the scope and standard of the software in other foreign languages. China would be a big loser in the information technology (IT) industry. Therefore China has to create a favourable environment at home to provide enough incentives for its own people to advance scientific and technology innovation, which is crucial to China's future status in international competition. The conclusion is that the protection of IPRs is not a favour for the foreigners; it is in the fundamental interest of China itself.

Secondly, China is currently launching a big campaign to address a serious market distortion that has become a major hurdle for China's economic development: the infringement of IPRs such as copyright piracy and trademark counterfeiting. China has adopted severe measures to crack down on intellectual property piracy, including the closure of manufacturing facilities as well as markets and shops that have been the object of administrative convictions for infringing activities.

IPR courts have been set up to hold those individuals and enterprises responsible for infringing activities and subject them to civil or criminal liabilities. In addition, Chinese administrative authorities have made special efforts to disseminate legal publications and enhance the education of the general public to create a favourable environment for enforcement. In this regard, international cooperation has played an important role. For example, since 1999, China and the European Union (EU) have been conducting successful IPR training courses for Chinese officials and specialists. The judicial and educational method has become part and parcel of China's major efforts to put its market in order, so as to direct Chinese reform towards achieving sound and rule-based goals.

Thirdly, in recent years, China has become a major destination of foreign direct investment (FDI), attracting US$40–45 billion a year on average. While facing the big challenge of maintaining its status as a premier location of inward investment among the developing countries, China is also improving the quality of the foreign investment.

By improving the quality of FDI, we mean, among other things, attracting more high-value investment with advanced technological content. This has been driven by the policy of gradually moving FDI from labour-intensive to high-value-added sectors.

In this connection, protection of IPRs has become a precondition for China to attract more FDI, especially in the high-tech area, as the preferential treatment provided in taxation and other incentives is not sufficient to maintain China's appeal to foreign investors.

The enforcement of IPRs will make China a stable, low-risk market, since infringement of IPRs has become a major risk for high-tech investment. What is more, the policy direction of the Chinese government of moving from labour-intensive FDI to high-tech FDI will also reduce the concerns of some neighbouring developing countries that China has diverted FDI from them. As a result, more FDI may go to those developing countries, which still enjoy advantages for the FDI that relies on low labour costs.

Fourthly, China has already started a process, which is still not that well known at this stage, of gradually making outward investment in other countries (the so-called strategy of 'moving out from China'). The legal environment, especially the extent of protection of IPRs in the countries targeted for investment, is already a major concern of Chinese investors.

China knows that only if China follows rules such as those of the WTO's TRIPs agreement, can their own investors be treated on the same terms. Even though China's outward investment is still low, its potential in the next decade could be enormous. And protection of IPRs in the host countries will be a strong incentive for China to invest abroad.

However, the Chinese government has realized that the enforcement of commitments in the IPR field might become one of the most difficult parts in its implementation of WTO obligations. This is because government commitment and a sound legal framework for IPRs would not suffice to ensure enforcement, as IPRs involve million of enterprises and hundreds of millions of individuals.

In order to achieve the goal of enforcement, a vigorous campaign of education is necessary. The Chinese government has already discovered that the 'benefit' generated from IPR infringement only goes to the individuals and enterprises responsible for these illegal activities. The illegal incomes stemming from the infringement are not taxed by the government and therefore do not contribute to the interest of the general public. Making the public at large more aware of this is part of the educational efforts that will provide a solid base for enforcement.

In addition to that, international pressure may prove to be an important actor. The dispute settlement mechanism of the WTO will be introduced, which will provide a strong measure for accelerated implementation of IPR laws and regulations. We are prepared to be part of this mechanism, as we are fully aware that the enforcement of the mechanism is in the fundamental interest of everybody.

8

WTO, Globalization and New Technology: Changing Patterns of Competition and New Challenges for Sustainable Industrial Development

Supachai Panitchpakdi

Globalization is often described as the process of increasing the integration of the world economy of countries becoming more interdependent and interconnected. As we embark on the twenty-first century, advances in information and communication technologies (ICT) are helping pave the way for greater economic integration through unprecedented rapid flows of goods, services, capital and ideas. Each day, more than US$1.5 trillion is traded in the global currency markets; each year nearly a fifth of the goods and services the world produces are traded internationally. Much has been said about how globalization has helped to realize the benefits of free trade through comparative advantage and division of labour. There is also supporting, although not uncontroversial, evidence of a link between external openness and economic growth via greater access to technology.

As we enter the new millennium, we find ourselves in an era of knowledge-based economies where the possession, distribution and consumption of knowledge play an important role in economic growth. Competitiveness is becoming more dependent on human capital and the acquisition of technology. In order for least-developed countries (LDCs) and developing countries to avoid falling further behind the more advanced economies, they must be able to bring and apply information, ideas and innovations from abroad.

Foreign direct investment (FDI) and international trade are useful instruments for this transmission of knowledge and technology. When we buy a foreign product that we cannot produce ourselves, we can learn about the innovations it contains, and perhaps one day manufacture it ourselves. When a transnational corporation opens an overseas plant, the host country can learn from the technological know-how that is brought in. This will improve the local workforce and enable them to acquire skills that they would never have gained if the plant had not been based there. These are good examples of how openness in foreign trade and investment can bring opportunities to improve human resources. Clearly, globalization has its virtues. However, there are many critics who observe that the acceleration of globalization is accompanied by a sharp increase in economic inequalities. Many less advanced economies are often at risk of being at the receiving end of the disadvantages of globalization. That the fruits of globalization are not shared evenly is evident enough: more than 1.4 billion people around the world are struggling to get by on less than US$1 a day; one-third of the children in developing countries are plagued with malnutrition; and an estimated 900 million people are either unemployed or under-employed. Moreover, the LDCs account for less than 0.5 per cent of the world's exports and they receive less than 1 per cent of the world's total FDI.

Not too long ago, the UN Secretary-General, Kofi Annan, stated that 'the main losers in today's very unequal world are not those who have been exposed too much to globalization. They are those who have been left out.' A good example of this can be found in the area of information technology (IT), in what has come to be known as the Digital Divide. At present, less than 5 per cent of the total world population of six billion have access to the internet. Sadly, only 10 per cent of these Internet users are in the developing countries.

At the G-8 meeting held in Okinawa on 22–23 July 2000, the industrialized countries acknowledged the seriousness of this problem and pledged to help make the opportunities derived from the global information economy as broadly available as possible – from the richest to the poorest nations. Improving the availability and affordability of the Internet in the less-advanced nations will certainly be a key instrument and effective means to bridge the technology gap between the North and the South. The IT sector, which provides the infrastructure that makes electronic commerce possible, can assist developing countries in expanding their share of international trade.

The World Trade Organization (WTO) has paid full attention to the changing demands in the twenty-first century and it recognizes the vital importance of IT and its roles in economic development and growth. This rule-based organization is determined to remove any barriers to developing the full potential of the Internet and IT. Indeed, the WTO has already equipped itself to meet this objective with its 1996 Agreement, the 1997 Fourth Protocol of Basic Telecommunications, the 1998 Work Programme on E-Commerce, and the Agreement on Trade Related Aspects of Intellectual Property Rights (TRIPs).

The role of the WTO

It is unlikely that the trend towards globalization will be reversed; the world in this millennium will certainly be even more integrated and more interdependent. The volume of international trade has been rising, and much of this is due to the combination of advanced ICT and the remarkable efforts of the General Agreement on Tariffs and Trade (GATT) and the WTO to dismantle trade barriers, both tariff and non-tariff, in the past eight rounds of multilateral trade negotiations.

The performance of the multilateral trading system under the auspices of the GATT/WTO over the past 53 years has assured us of its viability. The WTO is responsible for promoting the rules governing trade and creating new trade opportunities for its members. Since its inception, global trade has expanded seventeen-fold. Open trade under multilaterally accepted rules also helps provide global stability and predictability to our trading system. There is no denying that this system has contributed considerably to the overall growth of the world economy. While some people have expressed their doubts about the future of this organization after the débâcle in Seattle, it should be pointed out that at present there are almost 30 nations awaiting their accession to the WTO. In fact, the larger the number of countries involved, the greater the economic gains from multilateral trade negotiations through the exchange of concessions will tend to be. For the WTO to maximize its potential, it needs to have a membership that covers the whole world. No doubt, China's entry to this rule-based organization will serve this purpose, since its accession will bring most of the world's trade under the same multilateral rules and disciplines.

China's accession

Over the past 15 years, China has shown its strong determination to become a WTO member and has made many significant concessions on tariff reductions in several areas. The accession of China, with its 1.3 billion consumers, will offer many new market opportunities in sectors such as agriculture, industry, telecommunications, insurance and finance. Restrictions on business ownership will be eased for foreign investors, and China's membership will certainly bring greater balance to the multilateral trade negotiations.

Under WTO rules, there will be greater competition between Chinese firms and foreign companies, both in China's domestic market and on the world stage. Undoubtedly, this will require of China some necessary adjustments and structural changes. Although China will most likely retain its comparative advantages in labour-intensive industries, it will face greater difficulty in the areas of capital- and technology-intensive industries once exposed to fierce international competition. A dose of fair competition will heighten the pressing needs of many protected domestic companies to accelerate the improvement of their production processes and management quality. As in many other countries, including my own, many of China's state-owned enterprises are overstaffed and are not commercially viable. Thus, the nation will probably have to address this issue before being fully exposed to foreign competition. Fortunately, reformers will have more power and flexibility to reach their goals with these impending WTO obligations.

At present, the most competitive sectors or firms in China are those that receive little or no protection. On the other hand, telecommunications, insurance, banking and financial industries will have an arduous task to cope with the new environment, which the market-opening agreements will bring. In addition, the government will have to bring the country's regulatory environment in line with the WTO system: besides changing its current commercial practices, China will need to revise some of its laws and regulations to make them compliant with WTO rules.

Of course, accession to the WTO will bring China many opportunities as well as challenges, and the long-term benefits will outweigh the costs. Without a doubt, Chinese consumers will enjoy lower prices as well as a wider selection of goods and services, while Chinese producers and exporters will enjoy most-favoured-nation (MFN) status in the markets of all WTO member countries.

In the near future, China can expect a surge in FDI which will most likely be diverted from other countries in the region. With China offering greater transparency and predictability under the WTO rules and disciplines, many foreign firms will want to make their presence felt there by opening their branches or plants. Thus, China is likely to join many countries in the region in a shift from a rural and agrarian society towards a manufacturing-oriented one. Industrial restructuring as well as small and medium-sized enterprises (SMEs) will proliferate in China.

Making industrial development sustainable

It is undeniable that globalization and the WTO have helped accelerate the pace of industrialization worldwide. The average tariffs on manufactured goods in developed countries have been brought down from 40 per cent in 1948 to 4 per cent nowadays. Many developing countries have been the direct beneficiaries of this: the share of manufactured goods in their total exports has expanded significantly to 75 per cent. Accordingly, the share of employment in the industrial sector in these countries, in particular the newly industrializing Asian economies, has experienced significant growth as well. Even though job expansion in the service and knowledge-based sectors has grown more in the developed countries, the industrial sector will maintain its importance in creating employment in many of the developing countries. This demands that policy-makers pay full attention to formulating a sustainable industrial policy that will remain an integral part of the development strategies in their countries. Such a policy will include objectives in three areas: economic, social and environmental.

UNIDO and its technical cooperation programmes have been actively advocating the three dimensions of sustainable industrial development (competitive economy, productive employment and sound environment) in many developing countries. In principle, the WTO shares these same goals with UNIDO; however, we may have less flexibility in achieving these objectives. Even though we recognize the importance of a sound environment, we have our own mandate, namely, to serve as a multilateral trading forum whose objectives are to promote free and fair trade and use trade liberalization as a means to combat poverty, promote economic growth and increase employment. We must bear in mind that the WTO was specifically established to discuss trade issues.

The WTO and the non-trade issues

It is well recognized that the nations most integrated in the world community usually express greater concern about environmental protection. As income levels increase, their concern about the environment and the amount of resources available for environmental protection will rise as well. There is some empirical evidence suggesting that pollution increases at the early stages of development but decreases after a certain income level has been reached. This observation has been known as the Environmental Kuznets Curve (EKC). Hence, free and fair trade will elevate the living standards of the poor, which in turn can lead to a slowing down of environmental deterioration.

Yet, over the past few years, the WTO has been subjected to growing criticism from many non-governmental organizations (NGOs) and environmental groups that push for a linkage between trade and environment. Although trade liberalization probably creates some damage to our ecological system, it is safe to say that environmental problems have been exacerbated by the rise in industrialization, population growth and urbanization (with or without trade).

One should also acknowledge that the WTO is a member-driven organization. The organization itself does not make the global trade rules. Instead, the members who convene every two years at the ministerial meeting make these rules, which the organization upholds through its Dispute Settlement Mechanism (DSM) in the cases of disputes or violations of agreements. Since the mishap at the Seattle Ministerial Conference, the WTO members still remain at odds on various issues, because its decision-making process is based on each member having one vote. The opposing views of North and South on the trade–environment linkages are among the most controversial of these outstanding issues.

Developing countries and LDCs fear that non-trade concerns such as the environment and labour standards will be used by industrialized countries as another protectionist tool. It is the prevalent view of the developing countries that environmental standards are a function of the stage of development of the economy. Therefore, imposing upon them the same environmental standards that are applied in advanced economies, especially without financial and technical assistance, would raise their production costs and consequently weaken their comparative advantage in the export sector. Many developing countries also point out that rich countries are often guilty of causing most of the environmental damage (in per capita terms).

Imposing trade sanctions on less advanced economies, rather than solving the problems, will be counterproductive. Instead, greater market access, not less, will help raise living standards and improve environmental protection in these poor countries. The more affluent a country is, the better its chance to afford environmentally friendly technologies. Developing countries and LDCs are as concerned about the environment as the developed countries; they are, however, not in the same position as those more fortunate nations to adopt the same types of technologies or levels of measures. As a matter of urgency, they are faced with their more pressing needs to reduce their poverty levels, fight starvation and struggle to provide access to basic services such as education and healthcare with only limited resources.

The less advanced countries also argue that they are parties to a number of multilateral environmental treaties, and that it is within that framework that it would be most appropriate to deal with environmental issues. Indeed, there is a pertinent international organization: the United Nations Environmental Programme (UNEP). This said, the WTO is contributing in this area wherever it can. An ongoing work programme under the WTO's Committee on Trade and Environment (CTE) has been established in replacement of GATT's working group on Environment Measures and International Trade (EMIT), to analyze the relationship between trade and environmental issues in the promotion of sustainable development. In March 1999, the High-Level Meeting on Trade and Environment was held to enhance the dialogue between the WTO and civil society regarding this issue.

Some members have taken the initiative to improve the environment by tabling proposals to end harmful subsidies that promote industrial over-capacity. A new round of global trade talks can enable the dissemination of environment-friendly technologies around the globe by lowering tariffs on the environment-friendly sectors. Moreover, a new round could positively redress harmful subsidies, such as those maintained by some members for agriculture, fisheries and fossil fuels. The goals of the WTO are not only to ensure market liberalization but also to achieve sustainable development for all its members.

The twenty-first century will be full of opportunities and challenges. Technological advances will not only change our lifestyles, but also the ways we conduct business and the methods in which we produce goods. As industrialization is intensified in the era of globalization, the level of environmental deterioration will inevitably increase. Thus, the real challenge in the twenty-first century will be to find an agreeable global approach to achieve economic wealth and fair income distribution while attaining a healthy environment. But at the same time, we must respect each country's sovereignty in designing a regulatory framework for environmental protection that is appropriate for their own stage of development.

Low-interest financing for environment-friendly technologies from the international agencies to poor countries will enable the SMEs to afford the necessary equipment, while the strengthening of international cooperation in reducing poverty and granting technical assistance will be part of the solution.

9

Concluding Remarks on the Implications of China's Accession to the WTO for the Multilateral Trading System and Developing Countries

Long Yongtu and Carlos A. Magariños

FI4 019

P33 034

FI3 L67

China joins the WTO at a time when the multilateral trading system is besieged by a number of thorny problems and potential cracks, largely – but not exclusively – along North/South lines, which threaten to derail or at the very least considerably slow down the process of international economic integration.

The developed countries have their attention focused on liberalizing international exchanges to promote the knowledge economy. For them issues such as intellectual property rights, high value-added services, information technology, competition policies and free capital movements are at the top of the agenda.

For developing countries what matters most in this context is, first, to have fair competition and market access in those products where they have comparative advantage and, second, to have adequate access to technology inflows in order to advance towards higher value-added products. Free trade in labour-intensive products and unfettered access to their proprietary know-how is not a priority for the developed countries.

The matching between an approach to trade liberalization focused on fostering competition in frontier technological innovation and one centred around learning to compete on the basis of already existing technologies cannot be taken for granted. Although those issues of most interest to the developed countries are not necessarily of immediate concern for the developing countries, the way they are settled does impinge on their future development. On the other hand, although liberalizing agricultural and labour-intensive manufactures is not at all a key concern for the developed countries, it does bear upon developing countries' growth. Timeframes and priorities still appear to be worlds apart.

Nevertheless, a consensus appears to be emerging about the fact that the Uruguay Round agreements neglected an important dimension in the development of a rule-based system: to be able to comply with the agreements, two considerations have to be taken into account; that is, first, complying is not cost-free and, second, the cost entailed is simply beyond the reach of many developing countries. Setting up the necessary institutional and technical infrastructure, accessing the necessary information, understanding the issues involved and being able to negotiate them meaningfully is just *not* feasible for a large number of developing countries. This is *not* due to insufficient willingness or not good enough disposition; it results from a demonstrably genuine, sheer lack of domestic capability.

The so-called Doha Development Agenda[1] is intended as a roadmap to redress the hurdles in the globalization process by making the rule-based system more equitable and efficient.

At stake are such fundamental issues as addressing apparent fractures in the multilateral trade system along development lines and attaining the International Development Targets adopted in the Millennium Declaration, particularly that of reducing absolute poverty by 50 per cent by 2015.

Poverty reduction is not just a moral imperative. If market liberalization is to have any tangible meaning for developing countries, their markets need to be given the chance to develop by mobilizing capabilities and rising incomes. As the old Chinese adage goes, it makes no sense to kill a hen in order to get the eggs.

China and the multilateral trading system

What are the implications of China's entry in this context? May it be expected to contribute to bridge the lingering gap between the rich and the poor countries? Previous chapters have analyzed a number of dimensions of China's entry, as much from China's standpoint as from that of other developing countries – particularly the Asian emerging economies. Here we offer some preliminary thoughts on the questions posed in the previous paragraph.

China's accession to the WTO brings with it the expectation that developing country views and interests with acquire a greater voice.

Developing countries can be expected to gain a stronger presence in WTO to the extent that their interests coincide with China's. What is the scope of this coincidence? The following are among the core issues involved in this respect:

- Market opening and economic development
- Anti-dumping
- Textiles and clothing
- Intellectual property

Market opening and economic development

Although the nature of the issue differs across developing countries according to their initial conditions and actual level of development, China's insistence on the principle of prioritizing domestic market development in the context of progressive trade liberalization is entirely in line with the interests of developing countries. This is as much because of economic reasons as on social grounds – particularly that of poverty reduction. This point is likely to gain centre stage over the current round of negotiations *vis-à-vis* industrial countries.

But it also has an implication for economic relationships between China and other developing countries. Although in the short run there will be competition between them in labour-intensive manufactures, China's export mix is rapidly evolving towards increasingly higher technology products while the Chinese market is being increasingly opened to products where other developing countries, particularly those that come behind, have comparative advantages. These countries will therefore enjoy growing opportunities to expand exports to the Chinese market.[2]

Anti-dumping

Despite the apparent evenness of the revisions introduced by the WTO to the General Agreement on Tariff and Trade's (GATT) Article VI,[3] anti-dumping practices by industrial countries constitute a glaring example of sensitive issues for the developing countries. China fully shares the concern about fairness in the application of anti-dumping actions, all the more since it is particularly exposed in this regard (see Chapter 1). The ability to prepare and defend an anti-dumping case before the WTO's Dispute Settlement Panel (as in other cases) is another instance where the developing countries are at a clear disadvantage.

Textiles and clothing

Liberalization of trade in this area is definitely in the joint interest of China and that of the developing countries at large – their transient competitive benefits notwithstanding. China is hurt as much as the other developing countries by the back-loading of the process of liberalization through the Agreement on Textiles and Clothing, and is exposed to additional restrictions (see Chapters 1, 3 and 6). Furthermore, bilateral agreements prior to joining the WTO show that there is plenty of room for mutual understanding between China and other developing countries in this field with the aim of doing away with reciprocal trade frictions. A gradual relocation of labour-intensive activities, typically the production of textile and clothing manufactures, from China to other developing countries as incomes in China rise can also be expected.

Intellectual property

Drawing on foreign technology to mobilize domestic innovation and foster competitiveness upgrading is a priority for both China and the developing countries at large. Reaching equitable terms to facilitate access to proprietary technological assets by means of an intellectual property regime that encourages the transfer of technology rather than deterring it and lending itself to restrictive business practices is key to overcome lingering doubts about the implementation of the respective WTO agreement.

Looking forward

China is a developing country with per capita income under US$500. In line with China's definition of the poverty threshold, there are 30 million people who still live in poverty in China. By the UN standards – under US$1 per day – there are 230 million people still struggling below the poverty line. However, few doubt that China will continue its rapid pace towards catching up with the advanced industrial world – provided that trade frictions and market disruptions do not swamp the process – thus setting a new example of how globalization can be consistent with development and diminishing international disparities.

However, this would be largely an outcome from terms and conditions that resulted from a tough negotiation, not from the unfettered action of market forces – although these forces are no doubt one of the underlying driving forces of the whole process – the other being

China's vision on its own development process. China's WTO accession agreement is a clear example of pragmatism in the implementation of a shared will to materialize what was widely viewed as in the long-term benefit of all parties concerned.

For all the above reasons, China's WTO entry is good news for the developing countries – as well as for the world at large. This, however, should not lead to easy optimism. For instance, China's agreement sets very high standards for future entrants (particularly Russia), which issues a timely warning signal: they now need to work very hard and take maximum advantage from previous negotiating experiences to negotiate the best possible terms of entry.

Notes

1 This is what the agenda agreed at the Fourth Ministerial Conference in Doha, November 2001 is being called. For further details see http://www.wto.org/english/docse/legale/ursume.htm#fAgreement.

2 Even before joining the WTO China gave unconditional most-favoured-nation status to the majority of developing countries through bilateral trade agreements. Post WTO-entry China offers much lower tariffs and other favourable market entry terms to the developing countries at large.

3 For instance, greater clarity and more detailed rules were introduced in relation to the method of determining that a product is dumped, the criteria to be taken into account in a determination that dumped imports cause injury to a domestic industry, the procedures to be followed in initiating and conducting anti-dumping investigations, and the implementation and duration of anti-dumping measures. More specific provisions were also added on such issues as criteria for allocating costs when the export price is compared with a 'constructed' normal value and rules to ensure that a fair comparison is made between the export price and the normal value of a product so as not to arbitrarily create or inflate margins of dumping. Also, the requirement for the importing country to establish a clear causal relationship between dumped imports and injury to the domestic industry was strengthened.

Name Index

Subject Index